Peter Lucantoni and Lydia Kellas

Cambridge IGCSE®

English as a Second Language

Workbook

Fifth edition

CAMBRIDGE
UNIVERSITY PRESS

CAMBRIDGE
UNIVERSITY PRESS

University Printing House, Cambridge CB2 8BS, United Kingdom

One Liberty Plaza, 20th Floor, New York, NY 10006, USA

477 Williamstown Road, Port Melbourne, Vic 3207, Australia

314–321, 3rd Floor, Plot 3, Splendor Forum, Jasola District Centre, New Delhi – 110025, India

79 Anson Road, #06–04/06, Singapore 079906

Cambridge University Press is part of the University of Cambridge.

It furthers the University's mission by disseminating knowledge in the pursuit of education, learning and research at the highest international levels of excellence.

www.cambridge.org
Information on this title: www.cambridge.org/9781108465977 (Paperback)

First published 2018

20 19 18 17 16 15 14 13 12 11 10 9 8 7 6 5 4 3 2

Printed in Malaysia by Vivar Printing

A catalogue record for this publication is available from the British Library

ISBN 978-1-108-46597-7 Paperback

Contents

Menu

Introduction

The new edition of this Workbook is for students who are taking the Cambridge IGCSE English as a Second Language (E2L) examination, and it has been written to supplement the new edition of the Coursebook. It includes new material and new activities, to reinforce the language and skills from the Coursebook.

It is assumed that most of you who use this book will be studying English in order to improve your educational or employment prospects, and therefore it includes a broad range of topics and themes related to this goal. You will find passages and activities based on a wide range of stimulating cross-curriculum topics and about people from all over the world, which we hope you will enjoy reading and discussing.

This Workbook follows the same procedure as the Coursebook, with each unit focusing on a specific aspect of the IGCSE E2L examination, within the context of the unit theme. There are crosswords and word searches to help you with vocabulary, as well as grammar, and reading, writing and listening skills practice.

We hope you enjoy using this book!

Lydia Kellas & Peter Lucantoni

Unit 1

Free time

A Vocabulary

1 Look at the words below from Unit 1 and match them to make suitable phrases. More than one answer may be possible. **Example:** ***free*** **+** ***time***

~~free~~	resistance	scheme	game
shopping	creative	story	price
discount	board	training	app
online	loyalty	~~time~~	centre
amazing		puzzles	

2 Use the phrases from Exercise A1 to complete the sentences below.

Example: He was told to do his homework in his <u>free</u> <u>time</u> and not during school hours.

a In the examination you do not have to write a .... but to respond to emails and advertisements.

b At his gym they do a lot of .... because it improves muscle strength.

c In China, and other countries, they play this .... called 'Go' which uses white and black stones.

d .... are becoming more popular but not as much as the traditional paper ones.

e He downloaded this .... on his phone, so he can always find his car when it's in a car park.

f They're going to build another .... in our town; we've already got one huge one.

g If you join the company's .... then you'll get discounts on certain products all year round.

h The .... for these running shoes is $10 but you have to show your gym membership card.

3 Look at each of these groups of words from Unit 1. Which word in each group does not belong there? Write reasons for your answers.

Example: pencil <u>bag</u> pen sharpener
Bag is the odd one out because the other things you put in a pencil case.

a cardiovascular resistance training free weights general sports injury

....

b leaflet app newsletter programme

....

c creative funny delightful amaze

....

d someone birthday present basketball announced

....

e football tennis swimming cricket

....

f children adults couples boys

....

g shopping mall sports centre entertainment complex stalls

....

4 Complete the sentences below using one of the words from Exercise A3.

Example: They have built a huge <u>sports centre</u> at the Olympic park for the athletes.

a Before people used to shop at different shops but now they go to a ....

b .... is a great game played all over the world; however, it is known as soccer in the USA.

c A clown is supposed to be .... but they often frighten young children.

d In some countries .... learn to drive when they are 18 years old but in others it's 21.

e I love going to the marketplace and seeing all the different .... selling food and clothing.

f Yesterday they .... their engagement and plan to get married next year.

g We went to the cinema and saw a .... film which the whole family enjoyed.

h You can download this .... for free from the internet and it's really good.

5 Match each abbreviation with the correct unit of measurement. Then complete the sentences using the abbreviation.

~~millilitres~~	kilogram	kg	m
metre	kilometres	kph	GB
litres	Celsius	C	km
millimetre	kilometres per hour	cm	mm
centimetre	gigabyte	~~ml~~	l

Example: millilitres = ml You should only have put 100 <u>ml</u> of milk in that cake.

a You should drink about 3 .... of water each day.

b This USB stick has 19 .... of space left. Is that enough?

c The speed limit on motorways in many countries is 100 ....

d A bag of sugar normally weighs 1 ....

e Temperatures rise to about 45° .... in our country in the summer – it's very hot.

f A key on a laptop normally measures about 1 ....

g My daughter is going to run a marathon, so she runs about 5 .... every day to prepare.

h The shop is only about 100 .... away, I'm sure you can walk that far!

i On a map 1 .... doesn't look very far, but in reality it can be a very long distance.

6 Complete the sentences using *original* or *unique*.

a These jeans aren't really .... but they look the same and were much cheaper.

b A painting at the museum was stolen but they later found out that it wasn't the ....

c He has .... ideas that no one else has thought of but unfortunately none of them are practical, so they can't be used.

d You're not allowed to make copies from the .... so you have to buy a copy.

e She had the .... idea of going on a picnic on our day off – which is wonderful.

f Everybody has a(n) .... signature which sometimes is very difficult to understand.

B Language focus: phrases for preferences and suggestions, adjectives + nouns

1 Imagine that you are shopping with your friend. Complete the dialogue with preferences and suggestions.

Your friend: Do you like these shoes? I'm not sure about the colour.

You: I think the colour is lovely but you don't like them, do you? Try another colour. What do you think ....

Your friend: I don't know. I'm not sure about this shop. What do you think about .... (ing).

You: Oohh I don't know. I think I'd rather ....

Your friend: Yes, we could do but how about ....

You: I went there last week, so I'm a bit bored of it. I think we should ....

Your friend: Yes, that's a good idea!!! And we could walk home from there afterwards.

You: I suggest we .... and then we ....

Your friend: Oh, okay then. Whatever you want.

2 Read the following two blogs by teenagers talking about their free time. Find three adjectives + nouns in each blog and write them in the box.

Adjective	Noun
International	camel racing

a I'm from Oman and my country is very famous for camel racing. My father's sizeable family have been in the business of international camel racing for many years now and it is becoming increasingly popular. Camels used to be bred for their delicious meat and nutritious milk but nowadays their amazing speed is far more important. It's a very exciting sport and camels can be beautiful to watch from under the shade of the surrounding numerous date trees when they are running around the sandy tracks.

b I love swimming in my free time and I'm lucky as I've got an Olympic-sized pool near my house. I've been swimming since I was quite a young boy but now I get so much pleasure from it that I go swimming every day after school. I swim lengths up and down the empty pool for about an hour a day as everybody goes straight home, and then I go home, exhausted but ready to do my homework and eat a large dinner.

3 Now look at this third gapped paragraph. Complete it with information about yourself, and nouns and adjectives of your choice.

In my country, ..., a game that is very popular and one that is played by all ages is called .... It is mostly played by .... people but increasingly there are .... people who want to play because it is .... and .... People often sit ...., even in the .... weather, and either play or watch others playing. The game is .... but also .... and it has also become quite ....

4 Complete the sentences with a noun made from the adjective given.

Example: The man showed great generosity when he gave the old man a $20 note (generous).

a The audience greeted the musicians with much .... (warm).

b Her .... meant that she could organise her exam schedule well (efficient).

c He felt like a .... when he moved to his new school (strange).

d He looked with .... at the birthday cake his mother had made for him (delightful).

e He read the article about migrating birds with .... (fascinating).

f His .... for photography and drawing encouraged him to study art at university (enthusiastic).

g The driving instructor spoke to her with .... when she failed the test (firm).

h He made an .... when he delivered a speech on the environment (impressed).

C Skills

Reading

1 Look at the statements below, which will help you to revise about reading. Are they true or false? If 'false' then give the correct answer.

a *Skimming* is used to quickly identify the main ideas of a text.

....

b *Scanning* is used to find key ideas and words in a text.

....

c It is usually necessary to understand all words in a text to find answers to questions.

....

d You are always required to write a full sentence for your answers.

....

e Numbers must be spelt correctly to gain full marks for a question.

....

f You need to add a symbol or unit of measurement if you are referring to a quantity.

....

g It is a good idea to underline key words in a text.

....

2 Remember: before you answer questions from a text, it is important to know what you are looking for. Underline the key words in the following questions.

a What are the six ways that can help a person become successful?

b What is the minimum recommended daily exercise?

c What kind of books will improve your skill of reading?

d Other than at school and college, where are good places to learn?

e What are two examples of how you can help other people?

f Why is it not healthy to only focus on your studies?

g What people should you always give priority to in your life?

h Is it important to include all of the points listed in order to be successful? Why/not?

3 Write down the type of answer that each of the questions in Exercise C2 requires.

Example: a Six words or phrases.

b ....

c ....

d ....

e ....

f ....

g ....

h ....

4 Now read the text about six different ways of being successful, then answer the questions from Exercise C2.

How people spend their free time can have a big impact on their success as a person. Successful people tend to spend their free time in these six ways (and more, of course), so read below and find out why:

1 They Exercise. Physical exercise is important for both physical and mental health. Taking at least half an hour's exercise a day can get your blood pumping and revitalise your spirit. Exercising regularly also helps you remain disciplined, which can be valuable in an everyday environment, and can reduce the long-term effects of stress as well – meaning regular exercisers tend to be less stressed about their lives. You'll also look better and feel better, which gives you greater confidence.

2 They Read. Reading is a lifelong skill, and successful people never stop reading new books. Whether it's fiction or non-fiction, books help give you a greater understanding of the world around you. They introduce you to new characters, new environments, new cultures, new philosophies, and new ideas. Similarly, reading regularly helps to build your vocabulary and your semantic comprehension, giving you greater communication skills.

3 They Take Classes. Education shouldn't stop at school or college, and shouldn't be restricted to institutions. The most successful people in the world are the ones who make a commitment to never stop learning. They're always incorporating new skills for their CVs and learning new aspects of the world around them. Many local colleges offer courses for free. So don't underestimate the value of free online courses – if you have a free hour and an internet connection, you can start learning a new skill.

4 They Volunteer. Volunteering, no matter where or how you do it, is beneficial for you and your community. Whether you're helping to clean up a highway, working in a soup kitchen, or providing support to young people, your time goes a long way toward improving the community around you. Volunteering is also a valuable networking experience, introducing you to other people like you.

5 They Have Hobbies. Focusing exclusively on work or school might seem like a fast track to success. With nothing else distracting you, you can funnel your full effort into this and do in one week what would take most people two. But this approach has a nasty downside; it stresses you out and prevents you from developing skills in any other areas. Finding and pursuing a hobby, on the other hand, helps you relieve stress, put your life in perspective, and builds skills that complement ones you use every day. It's a breath of fresh air that keeps you grounded, and involved with other people.

6 They Spend Time With Friends and Family. This is the last point, but again your job or school isn't everything. Focusing too much on what you want to achieve is self-sabotage, no matter how counterintuitive that might sound. If you want to be successful in life, you have to prioritise your personal relationships – your bond with your friends and family members. No matter how much you want to be successful and develop, you shouldn't neglect your friends and family to do it.

If you don't spend your free time like this, it doesn't mean you have no chance of being successful. However, picking up some of these strategies can improve your abilities, improve your mindset, and expand your network to levels that will increase your chances for success in life. Start incorporating a few of them into your free-time routines and you might just be surprised at the results.

a ....

b ....

c ....

d ....

e ....

f ....

g ....

h ....

5 Find words which match with the definitions:

a Relating to the body of a person instead of the mind. ....

b A feeling or belief that you can do something well or succeed at something.
....

c An established organisation. ....

d To think that something is smaller or less important than it is. ....

e Fail to care for properly. ....

f To include. ....

D Writing

1 Read the text in Exercise C4 and then imagine your teacher has asked you to write about how **you** spend **your** free time. Write two/three paragraphs, about 100 words.

Include the following information:

- Say whether or not you agree with the comments.
- Describe how you personally deal with each of the issues.
- Add any other areas that you feel would make a person successful.

....

....

....

....

....

....

....

....

....

....

....

Unit 2
Television

A Vocabulary

1 Match each type of TV programme to its description.

Programme		Description	
a	~~Soap~~	**i**	Often longer than TV programmes and normally made for cinema
b	Documentary	**ii**	Where games are played by the general public, often for prizes
c	News	**iii**	Documents everyday people in real-life situations with unscripted dialogue
d	Quiz show	**iv**	Where a presenter talks to famous people about their lives
e	Chat show	~~**v**~~	~~Follows the lives of people where the story is often dramatic and unrealistic~~
f	Reality show	**vi**	Looks in detail at events of the week, typically politics
g	Series	**vii**	A daily report of the day's events, both nationally and internationally
h	Film	**viii**	Has factual information about life, whether animals, people, space, etc.
i	Current affairs	**ix**	Same situations and people with different or continuing story week to week

Example: (a) Soap (v) Follows the lives of people where the story is often dramatic and unrealistic.

a .... f ....

b .... g ....

c .... h ....

d .... i ....

e ....

2 Choose four of the most popular programmes in your country. Say what type of programme it is and its name. Then write if you watch it and why/why not.

Example: Soap – Friends. I don't watch it as I don't find the humour funny.

a ....

b ....

c ....

d ....

3 Make compound nouns with the following words, then complete the sentences. Some gaps may have more than one correct answer and there is one compound noun that you don't need to use.

mobile	information	leaflet	media
voluntary	sound	phones	money
social	smart	programme	system
television	pocket	standards	work
living		phones	

a My children receive .... every month for doing jobs around the house.

b It's always difficult to know which .... are best as there are so many different types out there.

c She does .... every week because she finds working every day in an office unrewarding.

d .... have changed so rapidly over the years and now we can't imagine living without them.

e They had to buy an additional .... as the one on the television was not very good quality.

f Overall .... have risen throughout the world but still there are many discrepancies.

g Advertising on .... is not the same as putting adverts in shop windows and in the newspaper like it was about ten years ago.

h .... are a good way to get across a summary to people but they can't go into detail.

4 Complete the sentences using *obviously* or *apparently*.

a They .... need to plan it in advance as they have the children to think about.

b The concert went very well last night ...., but I wasn't there to hear it.

c Well .... we'll have dinner before the cinema, as otherwise it'll be too late to eat.

d ...., they're having lots of money problems according to my friend at the bank!

B Language focus: adverbs

1 Unscramble the letters to make adverbs. The first letter is given.

Example: zaagmyinl = amazingly

a ylefbautiul = b..

b mceployetl = c ....

c foulbdytul = d ....

d ueaenytllv = e ....

e nfbayhisoal = f ....

f nsgeeryoul = g ....

g nhyguril = h ....

h ccorrynietl = i ....

2 Use the words from Exercise B1 to complete the sentences.

- **a** The teacher .... marked the tests, so they got lower grades.
- **b** They .... finished the race after a lot of effort.
- **c** The dog ate the food ....
- **d** They were .... surprised by his reaction to the comment.
- **e** She listened to his excuses .... as he always lied.
- **f** He was very .... dressed and looked professional.
- **g** Everyone was asked to give .... to the charity.
- **h** She finished off the letter .... with her signature.

3 Now write sentences using each of the adverbs below.

Example: astonishingly – Astonishingly he finished the race first despite his health issues.

- **a** fabulously ....
- **b** interestingly ....
- **c** horrendously ....
- **d** supposedly ....
- **e** greatly ....
- **f** extremely ....
- **g** carelessly ....
- **h** presumably ....

C Skills

Reading

1 You are going to read an internet article: 'The state of television worldwide' (on the next page). Find and underline the following words/phrases (a–h) in the text and then match them to their meaning (i–viii).

a	Digital revolution	**i**	Amount of money you pay regularly to receive a product or service
b	Medium (noun)	**ii**	A wireless method of updating new software to mobiles and tablets
c	Milestone	**iii**	A significant stage or event in the development of something
d	Over-the-air	**iv**	Wires used for transmitting electricity or telecommunication signals
e	Subscriptions	**v**	The change from mechanical to electronic technology
f	Retailers	**vi**	Television companies that make money by advertising
g	Cable	**vii**	A particular form or system of communication
h	Commercial television	**viii**	People that sell goods to the consumer

2 According to the text, are the following statements (a–g) true or false? Give reasons for your answers and say in which paragraph you found the information.

a More than 50% of the world's households own at least one television.

....

b A major change happened throughout the world in how we receive television signals.

....

c Free over-the-air television is now the most popular form of transmission.

....

d The developed world own fewer televisions due to limited access to electricity.

....

e Sales in televisions are expected to fall further.

....

f How we understand the definition of 'television' is set to change in the future.

....

g Television is expected to remain the main way people get information.

....

The state of television worldwide

As we witness the evolution of what we still call 'television', it's always useful to put it in the context of how the rest of the world views this medium. The rate of adoption varies from country to country but the digital revolution passed a milestone recently.

That milestone involved the adoption of digital TV. For the first time, more than half of the world's population with TV sets are now within reach of a digital TV signal. The figure stands at approximately 55% as of 2012, compared to just 30% in 2008. The adoption rates vary from an estimated 81% of the total number of households in first world countries to 42 per cent in the developing world.

More people worldwide now pay for their TV than get it over-the-air. At the end of last year, there were a total of 728 million pay-TV subscriptions. The adoption rate increased 32% between 2008 and 2012 and now stands at 53%, surpassing free over-the-air TV in 2011.

Globally, more than 1.4 billion households now own at least one TV set, representing 79% of total households; it is noted that 'virtually all' households in the developed world now own a TV set while 69% own at least one set in developing countries. In Africa in particular, fewer than a third of the households own a TV set; one of the main reasons for the low rate is the limited access to electricity.

Nonetheless, many retailers worldwide have low expectations as shipments of TV sets continue to decline. Accordingly, 2013 will mark the second straight year of lower shipments and this year the forecast is to fall by 5% (2012 saw a 7% decline).

When considering how to evaluate all these statistics, we have to remember that the actual definition of television is rapidly changing, especially in the developed world. Will the rapid growth of smartphones and tablets mean continued softness in TV set sales, particularly among the young? How countries handle the television marketplace varies widely, from countries like the United States and Brazil where commercial television dominates the landscape to other areas where government controls the market. These factors cannot be ignored when considering such changes.

One thing is certain though: for the foreseeable future, television will continue to dominate how the world's population gets its information and entertainment, whether it be over-the-air, cable, satellite or whatever other means. But one thing we do know is its importance cannot be understated and there's no going back.

Adapted from: http://www.tvtechnology.com

D Writing

1 You have been asked to choose two programmes for your national television and to schedule them. Write to the national television authorities and explain why you chose those particular programmes and why you scheduled them at the times you did.

Before you write your letter think about the following points:

- Times of the programmes
- Who your audience is
- Name/title of the programme
- A brief description of the programme
- Type of programme, i.e. sport, soap, etc.

Unit 3
Food

A Vocabulary

1 Write a type of food for each letter of the alphabet. Use a reference source where necessary.

a Apple .... **n** ....

b .... **o** ....

c .... **p** ....

d .... **q** ....

e .... **r** ....

f .... **s** ....

g .... **t** ....

h .... **u** ....

i .... **v** ....

j .... **w** ....

k .... **x** ....

l .... **y** ....

m .... **z** ....

2 Put the words from Exercise A1 into categories. Some words may fit into more than one category.

Fast food	Traditional food	Neither
	Pasta	

3 Complete the table with words that you used in Unit 3. You will find the name of a vegetable in the centre column.

neglected / supposing / insist / ~~batch~~ / registers / cabinet / increase / target / donate

						b	a	t	c	h				

4 Use the words from Exercise A3 to complete the following sentences. You may need to change the form of the word.

Example: The last <u>batch</u> of jam was not as tasty as the previous one.

a The children were asked to .... some money to buy food for the victims.

b The company sets very high .... in all its restaurants internationally.

c They .... that all children wear the full uniform and exceptions cannot be made.

d There has been an .... in the number of children who are bullied at schools.

e The animal had been .... and was in need of medical attention.

f You will find the First Aid kit in the .... in the bathroom.

g Supermarket checkout .... are being replaced by automatic scanners.

h '... he doesn't get that job in the restaurant, could he apply at your place?'

5 Circle the correct word in each sentence.

a I **insist / persist** that you tell me what you were told by the Headmaster.

b She should **insist / persist** that they pay her something towards the upkeep of the house.

c If he **insists / persists** in eating that rubbish, then he's definitely going to put on weight.

d Normally they just let us leave early but sometimes they **insist / persist** that we stay on late.

e They really should **insist / persist** that they continue the lessons, as they've been paid for now.

f I think you should **insist / persist** in asking for the repayment as it's not fair that they don't give it to you.

B Language focus: *providing, as soon as, supposing, to*-infinitive

1 Match the sentences and then rewrite a complete sentence using either: *providing* or *as soon as* or *supposing*. Remember these can be used instead of *if*. See the example to help you.

a	.... they don't come,	**i**	I knew they didn't want to come with us.
b	We'll leave the house	**ii**	.... they come so we're not late.
c	We should get there on time,	**iii**	.... ~~he eats all those sweets~~.
d	.... they told me,	**iv**	then we'll have to go without them.
e	I think we've taken the right clothes,	**v**	but that's .... the weather is good.
f	We'll definitely go and celebrate	**vi**	.... that there's not too much traffic.
~~**g**~~	~~The child will be sick,~~	**vii**	.... you pass your driving test.

Example: The child will be sick, if he eats all those sweets.

a ....

b ....

c ....

d ....

e ....

f ....

2 Write questions with these mixed-up words using *to*-infinitive. Underline the *to*-infinitive clause and then write an answer for each of the questions.

Example: walk why for it so does school take long you to to?
Why does it take so long for you to walk to school? Because I'm a slow walker.

a rice rice does cook take brown white it longer to than?

....

b write long it how take essay you to an does?

....

c time do what you breakfast up to eat get?

....

d study you do each like where to day?

....

e with do you watch sit down to when family television your?

....

f grammar we do study have why to?

....

3 Write two sentences for each situation given. Each sentence should include the *to*-infinitive clause.

Example: Cooking and eating at home.

a *It is a good way to check and control what you are eating.*

b *The best food to eat is food cooked at home.*

Eating in a fast-food restaurant.

a ....

b ....

Eating in a traditional restaurant.

a ....

b ....

The sale of fizzy drinks.

a ....

b ....

C Skills

Reading

1 You are going to read a text about obesity. Read and choose a heading from the box for each paragraph. There is one heading you will not need.

Worldwide trends
Health dangers of obesity
Statistics on the sales of fattening foods
Not just what you eat
Shoppers' habits
Sales of healthier products
Obesity – fat of the land

a ....

Governments are under pressure to change the way people eat, although it already seems that diets are changing. Unfortunately, there is more resistance with younger consumers, as peer pressure tends to have more impact than any amount of government intervention. Given mankind's need to worry, it is not surprising that the diseases of prosperity – stress, depression and, increasingly, obesity – get a lot of attention. The fact is that obesity, which is a preventable disease, is a serious problem, as it increases the risk of diabetes, heart disease and cancer and is the fifth leading risk for global deaths.

b ....

Over the past two decades obesity has been much researched and statistics have shown an alarming inclination with a constant upward growth in most regions of the world. Obesity has more than doubled since 1980:

- 39% of adults aged 18 years and over were overweight in 2014, and 13% were obese.
- Most of the world's population live in countries where being overweight and obesity kill more people than being underweight.
- 42 million children under the age of 5 were overweight or obese in 2013.

Of these and according to gender:

- 74% of men were overweight or obese.
- 64% of women were overweight or obese.
- Equal percentages (36) of men and women were obese.
- Among men, 4% were extremely obese. The percentage among women was double that of men, at 8%.

It is not clear what governments can do about it, and evidence suggests that the idea of imposing taxes on foods is not necessarily the answer: in Sweden, where advertising to young people is already banned, children are as overweight as they are in any comparable country. In fact, about one-third of children and adolescents aged 6 to 19 were considered to be overweight or obese and more than 1 in 6 children and adolescents aged 6 to 19 are considered to be obese. Obesity is also seen as a class issue, with more than 30 million overweight children living in developing countries and 10 million in developed countries.

c ....

But, despite the statistics, there is an obvious change that is happening worldwide. Shoppers' behaviour suggests that an opposite trend is developing. It is not just the flight from carbohydrates; there is a broader shift going on.

d ....

Companies are edging away from fattening foods. Five years ago, chocolate made up 80% of sales in a world leading company, now, that is down to half. Five years ago, 85% of drinks sales were sweet, fizzy stuff. That's down to 56%. The rest is mostly juice. Diet drinks – which make up a third of the sales of fizzy drinks – are growing at 5% a year, while sales of the fattening stuff are static.

e ....

Supermarkets say that people are buying healthier foods. Lower calorie ranges grew by 12% in 2003: twice the growth in overall sales. Sales of fruit and vegetables are growing faster than overall sales too. Cafés and restaurants also report an increase in healthy eating. A sandwich store says that sales of salads grew by 63% last year.

f ....

But it isn't just eating too much fatty stuff that makes people fat. It's laziness too. That may be changing. According to a market research company, there were 3.8 million members of private gyms last year, up from 2.2 million in 1998. The average man got thinner in 2012.

2 Read the article again and answer the questions.

a What has more influence on what young people eat?

....

b What now kills more people than world starvation?

....

c What group of people tend to be more overweight than others?

....

d In Sweden, what's forbidden and what is the result?

....

e What suggests that there is change occurring?

....

f What are listed as the main culprits of weight gain?

....

g Give at least three examples of changes in people's habits.

....

D Writing

1 You want to start a campaign at your school to raise awareness of healthy eating. You have written to some major companies in the food industry to get information about the contents of their food products. Write an email telling your colleagues at school about your enquiries. In your email, you should explain:

- Who you wrote to and the focus of your enquiries
- What you are planning to do with the information
- The advantages you think your campaign might bring to the school
- How their help giving alternative ideas to raise awareness would be useful.

2 You want to start a campaign at your school to raise awareness about healthy eating.

Find **two** products in your home that you eat regularly:

a **one** local product, for example a fruit or a vegetable

b **one** imported product, for example a can of sausages or a box of chocolates.

- Research and list the nutrients in the local product.
- Make notes about the product's health benefits.
- Research the main ingredients in the imported product.
- Make notes about its benefits and possible harms.

Use your research and notes to write an article for your school magazine, raising awareness about healthy eating.

....

....

....

....

Unit 4

Transport

A Vocabulary

1 Find the ten words from the box in the wordsearch. An example has been done for you.

> bus / car / motorbike / balloon / train / ferry / bicycle / coach / boda boda / ~~aeroplane~~

U	C	F	B	K	F	B	D	Q	W	P	Z	K	Y	M
Y	J	L	F	Q	I	E	L	O	H	A	X	P	Y	I
X	R	G	L	C	Y	F	D	E	C	N	I	A	R	T
K	E	R	Y	E	M	E	K	V	A	W	X	P	Q	F
V	I	C	E	S	L	I	Z	Z	O	U	K	E	J	Y
B	L	H	U	F	B	T	E	X	C	H	M	H	A	X
E	O	B	A	R	B	R	C	G	K	I	Z	M	Q	I
F	J	D	O	O	A	E	E	J	A	H	G	X	I	A
L	P	T	A	T	L	**A**	**E**	**R**	**O**	**P**	**L**	**A**	**N**	**E**
M	O	A	D	B	L	N	C	P	C	A	R	G	Y	C
M	K	T	S	F	O	W	D	S	B	E	F	U	C	L
D	W	O	B	M	O	D	M	B	A	U	G	Q	S	I
W	I	D	W	G	N	N	A	X	A	W	V	W	Q	K
F	A	P	R	H	G	P	T	Y	V	O	J	C	S	W
M	V	Q	G	H	Q	S	R	G	D	A	M	Q	U	B

2 Choose which form of transportation from Exercise A1 is being described.

a It travels on water and carries people and goods, as well as vehicles.

....

b Many people drive one of these as their own personal form of transport.

....

c It has two wheels, no engine and normally only carries one person.

....

d It travels long distances by road, carrying large numbers of passengers.

....

e Not normally used as a form of aviation transport, but often used for entertainment.

....

f Normally transports people in a town, or short distances outside town.

....

g Has two wheels and an engine and is normally used to transport one person.

....

h Can cover long distances quickly and efficiently with many passengers.

....

i Has changed the world with international travel.

....

j Can be a dangerous form of transport and is only found in certain countries.

....

3 Complete the sentences using either *catastrophe(s), catastrophic* or *disaster(s)*.

a The damage done to the roads after the massive earthquake was a complete ....

b One of the worst .... I can remember is when my car was crashed into.

c Tsunamis and earthquakes can have .... effects on the economy of a country, which can take years of recovery.

d It'll be a .... if the main speaker doesn't arrive on time for the presentation.

e People donated a lot of money after the .... in Asia.

f My speech was a complete .... as I forgot my notes and the microphone wouldn't work.

4 First make pairs of the following words and then use both words to complete the sentences below.

livelihoods	divorce	river	fatalities
~~Olympic~~	strain	roads	initiative
people's	~~slogan~~	participants	women
potholed	common sense	marathon	
swelled	campaigned	accident	

Example: The <u>Olympic slogan</u> is 'Higher, Faster, Stronger'.

a The .... are so badly .... that they are damaging my car.

b The .... to dangerous levels that night after the rain.

c It's not always possible to compare .... as so many factors are involved.

d A lot of .... was put on the family after the ....

e There were many .... after the .... on the motorway.

f .... have .... for equal rights in many countries.

g If you use your ...., imagination and ...., then you should be fine.

h There was a surprisingly high number of .... for the..

B Language focus: tenses review, nouns and verbs

1 Read the following story. How many different tenses from Unit 4 Section D can you see? Find and write examples of each one below:

a Present perfect simple ....

b Past simple ....

c Present continuous ....

d Future simple ....

Last month I travelled to Uganda for the first time and I should've been met at the airport by the hotel taxi. But for some reason, the taxi wasn't waiting for me and there I was, waiting, getting hotter and hotter in the afternoon sun, when this man came walking up to me and politely asked if I needed help. I've always avoided talking to strangers, but as he looked at me with a big grin on his face, I just couldn't resist talking to him.

'I've got a taxi booked,' I told him, 'but it hasn't turned up.'

He looked at me and said:

'Mr Sir, "Help" is my first name. You need some transport to get you to the place you're staying at now. Am I right?'

I smiled back at him and nodded, and asked what he was offering. He asked me where I was going, and to go with him with the warning:

'Outside will be very hot and busy, so you stay with me.'

So I ventured from the quite noisy airport arrivals lounge to the noisy exterior and was faced with a mass of bustling, pushing, crazy humanity. My friend firmly took my arm and luggage and led me towards a seemingly endless line of motorbikes of all types and descriptions. There were new ones, old ones, big ones, small ones, dirty, clean, shiny, damaged ones, anything-you-can-imagine ones. My friend took me to his motorbike and with his arms open wide said:

'Here, Mr Sir, is your taxi, your boda boda taxi, and look, you have even got a helmet. We'll get you to your hotel nice and safe, don't you worry about a thing.'

I looked at him in disbelief, thinking how am I going to get on that with all my luggage? But as I looked around me I was stunned by what I saw and realised that my boda boda was just one of many boda bodas that transported absolutely anything and anyone, anyplace and anytime.

He carefully made me sit and balanced my luggage on my knee, and with a flourish sat the helmet on my head. He asked:

'Are you sitting comfortably, Mr Sir? Then off we go.'

And so began my first great boda boda adventure in Uganda. I know that I'll write my many stories about the different experiences I've had and I know I'll definitely go back to Uganda to look for my friend 'Help'.

2 Change the following *-ion* nouns into verbs.

Example: collision → collide

Noun	Verb	Noun	Verb
decision		protection	
expression		examination	
admission		suggestion	
cancellation		subtraction	
education		graduation	

3 Choose three noun/verb pairs from the table above and use them in meaningful sentences of your own.

Example: Education is very important to my parents and they want the best for me.
He only agrees to educate children who are really keen.

a ....

....

b ....

....

c ....

....

C Skills

Listening

1 Look at these exam-style questions. Write down what type of information each question requires you to listen for.

a **i** What can happen to many foreigners in Kampala? ....

....

ii What is recommended for safety on a boda boda? Give two details. ....

....

b **i** Why did the narrator hold on to the driver? ....

....

ii Where were the mother and her baby being taken? ....

....

c **i** Why did the narrator ride with Dennis? ....

....

ii Where did they go on day three? ....

....

d **i** How did the narrator feel when she began working? ....

....

ii What does she need to be careful of when driving? Give three things. ....

....

2 **CD2, Track 18** You are going to hear four people talking about their experiences with a boda boda. Listen and answer the questions in Exercise C1 with short answers.

a **i** ....

ii ....

b **i** ....

ii ....

c **i** ....

ii ....

d **i** ....

ii ....

D Reading

1 You are going to read about some unusual types of transport from around the world. Before you read, look at this type of unusual transport and complete the sentences about it.

balancing	police	battery	American	Segway®

a It's called a ....

b It is self- .... unlike a bicycle.

c It is used in various countries by the ...., security personnel and tourists.

d It is a ....-powered, electric vehicle.

e It was invented by an .... called Dean Kamen in 2001.

2 Now answer these questions about a Segway.

a Have you seen a Segway? ....

b Would you like to drive a Segway? Why/why not?

....

....

c In what ways is a Segway different from traditional vehicles? Write your ideas below.

i ....

ii ....

iii ....

3 Now read about the different forms of transport and answer the questions that follow each one.

Getting around abroad doesn't have to be all about cars, trains, buses and bikes. From cruising Peru's Lake Titicaca on a boat made of reeds to flying down the streets of Madeira in a wicker toboggan or taking an odd horse-drawn carriage in Pakistan, there are so many unusual types of travel to be tried. Here are some of the best.

Traghetto, Venice

Along the 3.5 km stretch of Venice's Grand Canal there are just three bridges, so how do you get across? By traghetto, of course. The unglamorous sibling of the gondola, these no-frills boats get passengers from one side of the canal to the other for a very small fee. You can pick up a traghetto (meaning 'ferry' in Italian) from any of the seven piers along the canal – just look for the yellow signs pointing you towards the landings. Each boat is rowed by two oarsmen, one at the bow and one behind the passengers, as in a gondola. If you want to ride like a Venetian, do not sit down for the short journey.

a Which other transport method is the traghetto compared to?

....

b Why might someone think you are a local if you stand up in a traghetto?

....

Tangah, Pakistan

Save yourself a few dollars in Pakistan and ride on a Tangah, rather than the more commonly used rickshaws and taxis. A Tangah is a carriage, sitting atop two large wooden wheels (not exactly designed for comfort, so expect a sore bottom on a long journey!), pulled by one or two horses. They have a low-glamour, but high-fun factor and have nowadays become more widely used in Pakistan for enjoyment, rather than as a functional way of getting around. Just beware that they're not the speediest way to travel!

c How can you spend less money in Pakistan?

....

d What are the disadvantages of riding in a tangah? Give **two** details.

....

Bamboo train, Cambodia

Those who are brave enough may want to ride a Cambodian bamboo train – known locally as a *nori*. Passengers sit on a makeshift bamboo 'train' (basically just a bamboo platform) powered by an electric generator engine, perched just inches above the railway tracks and travelling at up to 40 km/h. The unmaintained railway tracks make for a bumpy ride and the closest you'll get to luxury is sitting on a grass mat. But the fares are low and this is a once-in-a-lifetime experience, as all the locals use them for getting around. Pick up a *nori* from Battambang station.

e How does the *nori* move along the tracks?

....

f Why is the ride so uncomfortable?

....

Monte toboggan, Madeira

Monte toboggans arrived in the 19th century, as a fast way of getting down the hill from Monte to Funchal. Today, they're more a tourist attraction than an everyday mode of transport for the locals. Pick up a toboggan at the bottom of the stairs leading to the Nossa Senhora do Monte Church. Once you've climbed into the wicker sledge, two drivers dressed in traditional white outfits will steer you down the narrow, winding streets to Funchal at up to 48 km/h. It's an extraordinary and exhilarating experience.

From: www.roughguides.com

g What was the original use for the Monte toboggan?

....

h Who will help you to descend from Nossa Senhora?

....

Unit 5

Holidays

A Vocabulary

1 Use the code to find the words for the crossword in Exercise A2. All the words are from Unit 5 in your Coursebook.

Example: 3 1 13 2 18 9 4 7 5 = Cambridge

1	2	3	4	5	6	7	8	9	10	11	12	13	14	15	16	17	18	19	20
a	b	c	d	e	f	g	h	i	j	k	l	m	n	o	p	q	r	s	t

21	22	23	24	25	26
u	v	w	x	y	z

a 19 14 15 23 - 3 1 16 16 5 4 ....

b 16 1 18 1 13 15 21 14 20 ....

c 8 21 19 11 25 ....

d 16 15 16 21 12 1 18 ....

e 20 8 18 9 12 12 9 14 7 ....

f 22 15 12 3 1 14 15 ....

g 6 18 5 19 8 23 1 20 5 18 ....

h 16 18 15 6 5 19 19 9 15 14 1 12 ....

i 3 15 13 16 12 5 24 ....

j 5 14 4 5 13 9 3 ....

k 1 3 20 21 1 12 12 25 ....

2 Complete the crossword. The words in Exercise A1 are the answers to the clues.

Across

2 Very difficult or complicated (7)

5 More important than anything else (9)

6 A type of water that is drinkable and found in rivers and lakes (10)

9 Describes the white bit at the top of mountains (10 + hyphen)

10 Very exciting (9)

Down

1 A mountain that can explode and erupt (7)

3 Something or someone that is liked by many people (7)

4 Having qualities connected to trained and skilled people (12)

7 An adverb that can be used to show surprise (8)

8 Describes a plant or animal that is found in certain places (7)

11 A type of dog that can live in cold, snowy places (5)

3 Complete the sentences using either *stationery* or *stationary*.

a An easy way to remember *stationery* and *stationary* is to connect the *er* in .... to the pap*er* it's made of.

b Use the office .... to write a reply.

c They've opened a new .... shop near the university.

d The car was .... when it was hit by the man on the motorbike.

e Hold the dog in a .... position so I can take a picture of her.

4 Which adjective is the odd one out? Why?

Example: amazing spectacular dramatic unimpressive
unimpressive – all the other adjectives describe something positive

a rich wealthy needy affluent

....

b hungry satisfied starving famished

....

c noisy calm boisterous rowdy

....

d active busy idle working

....

e full complete entire lacking

....

f large insignificant huge immense

....

5 Complete the sentences using one of the words from Exercise A4.

a The children were very .... as the week started and hardly made any noise at all.

b Many world monuments are .... compared to the pyramids in Egypt.

c Only a small percentage of the world's population has great wealth but the vast majority are ....

d She has many great assets but is .... in one very important one – politeness.

e He is very .... and other than going to school, he just plays on his computer.

f He had just eaten a good breakfast and was so .... that he fell asleep.

B Language focus: compound adjectives

1 Pair the words to make compound adjectives and then use them to complete the gaps in the paragraph.

absorbing capped chocolate coloured leisure snow filled white pure shock

All the husky dogs had .... fur which showed up against the .... beauty of the freshly fallen snow. The dogs had to climb from the green fields of the lower hills to the peaks of the .... mountains. On their paws they wore

.... specially made leather boots, due to the pounding their legs would receive from the constant trekking. The dogs were used to a .... life living at ground level on the plains and rolling in the white sands of the freshwater lakes near their homes.

2 Make a compound adjective in the second sentence from the underlined information in the first sentence.

Example: Many of the roads in Britain are lined by trees.
There are many tree-lined roads in Britain.

a I live in a country where English is spoken. ....

b Shakespeare is an author who is known very well. ....

c She never cooks and only buys food that is already made and ready. ....

d He lives in a building which is 20 storeys. ....

e The cat is only two years old and already it's fat. ....

f The room is lit too brightly – I don't like it. ....

g She can only work part time because of the children. ....

C Skills

Speaking

1 Here are five examples of fillers from Unit 5. Write them out individually.

letmethinkactuallywelltobehonesthmm

2 **CD2, Track 19** Listen to Aphrodite talking to her teacher about the first part of her speaking exam. As you listen, note the order in which you hear the fillers, and how many times you hear each one.

3 **CD2, Track 19** Listen again. Write brief notes on what the teacher says to Aphrodite about each of the following.

a Worrying doesn't help

....

b The questions in Part One

....

c Using your own language

....

d Phrases to show you don't understand

....

e Not having enough to say

....

f The topic

....

g Pronunciation

....

h Mistakes

....

D Reading

1 Unscramble and rewrite these four pieces of advice on answering questions in the reading and writing papers.

- sections text search of likely the
- question read the
- word/s the underline key
- question ask asking information yourself the is for what

....

....

....

....

2 Underline the key word(s) in each of the following questions.

a How many methods of transport are available to reach the Isles of Scilly?

b What is *Scillonian III*?

c Name four 'treasures' of the islands.

d Which other part of the world are the islands compared with?

e How many people live on the Isles of Scilly?

f What do you need to do before travelling between any of the islands?

g On which island is the Old Wesleyan Chapel?

h Where can you find the second-oldest lighthouse in Britain?

3 Match words from the questions in Exercise D2 with the definitions below.

a Small islands. ....

b A small building for Christian worship. ....

c A tower or other tall structure to warn or guide ships at sea. ....

d A quantity of precious metals, gems or other valuable objects. ....

e Name of a place off the south-western coast of Britain. ....

f Something that carries people and objects from one place to another. ....

4 Read the text about the Isles of Scilly, then answer the questions from Exercise D2.

Discover the Isles of Scilly by air or sea

The Isles of Scilly Steamship Group provides you with two great choices to enjoy a day trip to the islands.

Whether you choose to cruise on *Scillonian III* or to fly on Skybus (the islands' own airline), and whatever time of year you visit, you will be sure to enjoy the natural beauty of the islands.

Exotic plants and wild flowers, ancient cairns and crumbling castles, sparkling white sands and an azure sea – all the treasures of the islands await you. Only 45 kilometres from England's Land's End, but with a real hint of the Tropics.

The Isles are populated by a community of 2000 islanders and there are five inhabited islands to explore to make your day trip one to remember. Inter-island launches are available from St Mary's quay. Check times and tides for availability.

St Mary's, where the airport is situated, is the largest of the islands. Hugh Town, its capital, is the commercial centre and offers a great choice of shops, restaurants and cafés. You will find the Tourist Information Centre at the Old Wesleyan Chapel in Hugh Town. Don't miss the exhibits at the museum or a walk round the Garrison and the Elizabethan fort, now known as the Star Castle Hotel. There are many walks, nature trails and safe white-sand beaches.

The other inhabited islands are St Martin's, Bryher, Tresco and St Agnes. On the latter is a 17th-century lighthouse, the second oldest in Britain, as well as an inn and a café for refreshments. The beaches at Porth Conger and the Cove are great for swimming.

a ....

b ....

c ....

d ....

e ....

f ....

g ....

h ....

Unit 6

Learning

A Vocabulary

1 Words that begin with 'g' 'c' 'p' and 'f'. Read through the definitions and fill in the missing words from Unit 6 of the Coursebook.

a A drawing that often shows numerical information g...

b The system and structure of a language g...

c A person who shows the way to others g...

d An adult educational institution c...

e Professional assistance in personal issues c...

f A lifelong occupation c...

g Earliest education p...

h A planned series of future events p...

i The way in which a word is said p...

j Things provided for a particular purpose f...

k Information discovered as a result of investigation f...

l A payment made to a professional person or body f...

2 Complete the sentences below with six of the words from Exercise A1.

a The .... at the school have gone up by 10% this year and are too expensive for us.

b Teaching and having good .... is a very important part of learning a new language.

c Going into a .... like medicine or law can take many years of hard study.

d His .... is really not very good but then he can communicate very effectively.

e They have organised a .... to take us around the old part of the town to tell us the history.

f The new sports centre has excellent .... and I think I'm going to join now.

3 Write complete sentences by matching phrases from columns A and B and including a location from the middle column.

A	Location	B
The students often go to the …	sports centre	… to relax and have a break.
You should go to the …	accommodation and welfare office	… if there is a problem with your flat.
There are good …	LMRC	… at the college, with ATMs everywhere.
~~On Sundays the~~ …	social and leisure programme	… ~~is closed, so download what you need today~~.
I felt very depressed about exams, so I went to the …	banking facilities	… and they really helped me.
I go every day to the …	~~IT centre~~	… to play table tennis.
You're not allowed to talk in the …	cafeteria	… because people study there.
We are always busy at the weekends as the …	counselling service	… is excellent and full of great activities.

Example: On Sundays the … IT centre … is closed, so download what you need today.

a ……………………………………………………………

b ……………………………………………………………

c ……………………………………………………………

d ……………………………………………………………

e ……………………………………………………………

f ……………………………………………………………

g ……………………………………………………………

4 Complete the sentences with either *practice* or *practise*.

a You need to ……………………… the language more to become fluent.

b If they ……………………… every day, they should be ready by next month.

c The law ……………………… has been taken over by different people now.

d What qualifications do you need to ……………………… as a doctor in the Philippines?

e He would like more ……………………… learning the guitar, as he loves it.

f ………………………! ………………………! ………………………! That's the only way you're going to learn.

B Language focus: prefixes and suffixes

1 Complete the sentences using the word stems in brackets. For each word, you need to add a prefix from the box and put the word into the correct tense.

mis- un- re- over- dis- trans- be- co- de- fore- ~~pre-~~

Example: Can you <u>pre+dict</u> the answer to the question? (-dict)

- **a** The dog tried to .... the boy in the park. (-friend)
- **b** Because she .... the instructions, she did the activity incorrectly. (-understand)
- **c** The exercise was .... and so she finished quickly. (-complicate)
- **d** They wanted to .... the area, as it was so beautiful. (-visit)
- **e** He missed the bus because he .... again after a late night. (-sleep)
- **f** She looked at him in .... because of the lies he was telling. (-belief).
- **g** If you .... better then you will finish the project quickly. (-operate)
- **h** Because the country's currency was .... prices rose drastically. (-value)
- **i** She was .... when she had her hair restyled. (-form)
- **j** They did not .... that the house would be destroyed during the hurricane. (-see)

2 Complete the crossword using some of the words from Exercise B1. You may need to change the form of the words.

Across

- **2** Completely change (9)
- **4** Refusal or reluctance to trust (9)
- **7** Simple (13)
- **9** Become someone's friend (8)

Down

- **1** Go to a place again (7)
- **3** Sleep for longer than you should (9)
- **5** Get something wrong (13)
- **6** Work with others (9)
- **8** Reduce or cancel the value of something (7)

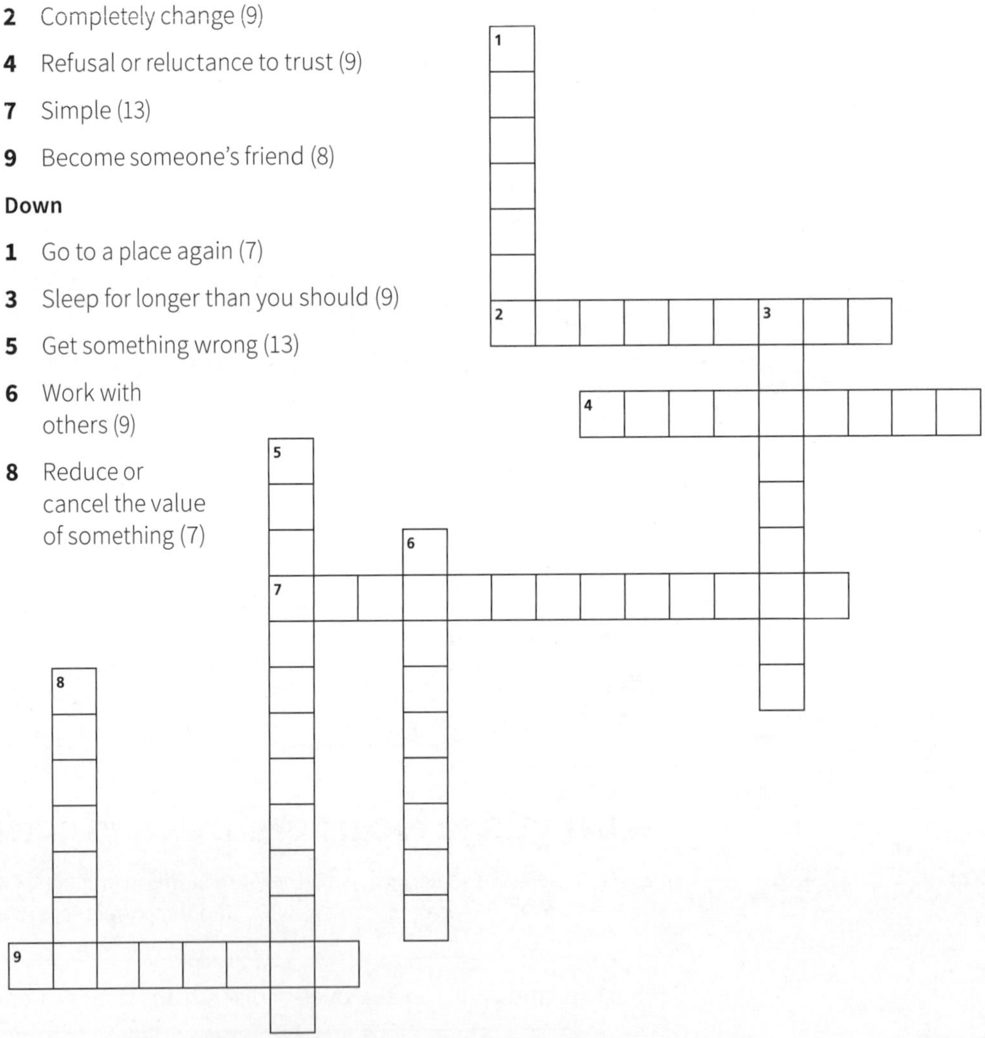

3 Underline the suffix in each word.

Example: accidental

a availability

b cheaper

c excitement

d guidance

e happiness

f imagination

g luxuriously

h loving

4 The following sentences sound strange. Rewrite the sentences, turning each of the underlined phrases into a word with a suffix.

Example: David painted the picture with great care.
David painted the picture carefully.

a Antoinette painted without caring.

....

b I wrote a letter full of gratitude for the lovely flowers.

....

c They saw a puppy without a home, wandering the streets.

....

d The painting is full of beauty.

....

e Big dogs, if looked after carefully, are without harm.

....

f Did you see the houses full of colour in that street?

....

g The car is without worth now that it has been damaged.

....

h The computer is of no use because it is so old.

....

C Skills

Reading

1 Read the article and choose which phrase from the box belongs in which gap.

can be so extreme	do physical damage	for hours on end
gaming addiction	in poor physical condition	more likely to suffer
infested with hostile creatures	on the verge of	to eat properly

What's the danger for video-game players?

You've been searching all day. You've travelled hundreds of kilometres, sometimes backtracking to make sure you haven't missed anything. Some areas are so **(a)** .... that you've been prevented from continuing on your journey until the creatures were destroyed. After all that, you've finally found what you've been looking for: the secret passage that transports you to another place: you've moved up to the next level! You've done it! You're so excited that you barely notice how much your back hurts, you don't notice that you are **(b)** .... getting a migraine headache again, nor do you realise that you haven't had anything to eat or drink all day.

It may sound like a strange story, but it's all too familiar for video-game players. Whether they play on an Xbox or online, they enter worlds filled with strange creatures by travelling to mysterious and sometimes secret locations. They spend so much time in this other world that they could begin to **(c)** .... to their bodies. Physical consequences of gaming addiction include carpal tunnel syndrome, migraines, backaches, eating irregularities, among other things.

Carpal Tunnel Syndrome (CTS)

CTS has long been associated with computer use, so it's no surprise that it's a physical symptom of **(d)** .... CTS is caused when the main nerve between the forearm and the hand is squeezed or pressed. This occurs when the carpal tunnel (the part of the wrist where the main nerve and tendons are located) becomes irritated or swollen. Overuse of a computer mouse can cause such irritation and swelling, as can excessive use of a video-game controller.

Migraines

Migraine headaches typically start in one spot and slowly spread, getting more painful as they progress. In severe cases, the pain **(e)** .... that it causes the sufferer to vomit. Both light and noise can cause excessive pain. Someone who plays video games for extended periods of time is **(f)** .... from migraines because of the intense concentration required and the strain put on the eyes.

Backaches

Backaches are a common physical symptom of gaming addiction because most gamers stay seated in the same position **(g)** .... The lack of movement causes stiffness and soreness, but could deteriorate into chronic back problems over a longer period of time.

Eating irregularities

Eating irregularities are caused by gaming addiction simply because most addicted gamers don't want to take the time **(h)** .... Rather than eating healthy, balanced meals, they eat food that is quick and usually unhealthy. In extreme cases, the gamer may choose not to eat at all.

These physical consequences may occur in varying degrees from one gamer to another and, of course, if a gamer is already **(i)** ...., they will be more susceptible to these effects.

From*: *www.video-game-addiction.org

2 Answer these questions about the text.

a What might prevent a gamer from continuing on their journey?

....

b Where might you go after finding the secret passage?

....

c Being excited means a gamer may not notice **three** things. What are they?

....

d Why can overuse of a computer mouse cause CTS?

....

e What might the physical effect be of intense concentration and eye strain?

....

f When could a chronic back problem occur?

....

g Why do many gamers eat unhealthy food?

....

h Which type of gamer is more likely to suffer physically?

....

D Writing

1 You have seen this announcement on posters in your town and school.

'Freedom in our computer lab' campaign

Parents complain about us sitting all day at the computer!

Now they are threatening to block the computers at our school – to control how we use them!

We don't only use the computers for gaming! We say respect our independence and intelligence.

We say allocate time for physical and computer activities. But don't completely control how computers are used in the lab.

Don't let this happen!

Write to your local newspaper expressing your opinions about the importance of allowing young people to use computers responsibly.

Find out more: ***www.complabcontrol.com***

2 Write a letter to a friend:

- giving reasons why time should be allocated for physical and computer activities at school
- explaining how your friends use computers responsibly
- giving suggestions of how the computers could and should be used at school.

Your letter should be 100–150 words long (Core) or 150–200 words long (Extended).

....

....

....

....

....

....

....

....

....

....

....

Jobs

A Vocabulary

1 The notes below each describe one of the jobs. Rewrite the notes by completing the words and making full sentences. Then identify which job is being described.

surgeon	teacher	~~pilot~~	engineer	police officer

Example: Works shift hrs & travels 2 many diff countries.
This person works shift hours and travels to many different countries. Pilot

a Many yrs at uni r nec 2 do job which can b v challeng and demand. They play a v import role in our society in looking after people & make them well.

....

....

b Uni ed v imp for this job. They play v imp role in our develop as adults & we learn many interesting thngs from them.

....

....

c Maintain peace & secur in our cities and wear unif so that can b easily identif. Men & w/men are both nec in this job.

....

....

d Do many diff jobs in the build and construct of city. Uni degr is extrem imp as so many areas 2 learn about.

....

....

2 Look at this example of linking words, which you saw in Unit 7 of your Coursebook.

Example: A teacher is a career which many students choose while at school.
Complete the sentences using the linking words below. There is one word you don't need.

also	in addition	sometimes	consequently
during	furthermore	besides	~~while~~

a The job of a teacher can be very satisfying, but .... it can be very challenging.

b In your career, you need to continue learning .... to teaching, if you want to develop as a professional.

c You are expected to fulfil requirements from your bosses .... those of your class.

d .... the workload can become quite stressful and performance can be affected.

e A good teacher is a dedicated one and .... one who loves their job.

f ...., a teacher is a person who, when asked, will give.

3 Put the linking words into the correct category in the table. There are two for each category.

in this case namely consequently in other words in spite of specifically
for this reason such as however for example as a result accordingly

Make clear	Contrast/ difference	Detail	Result/ consequence	Example	Summary

4 Complete the sentences using one of the words/phrases from Exercise A3. There may be more than one possible answer in some cases.

a I told you I'm not going. ...., I'm staying here!

b They painted the house, but more .... the upstairs bedrooms at the front.

c They say they don't go out much, ... being out every weekend.

d We've been told to bring lunch, ... a sandwich and a drink.

e He got a pay rise and .... they are going on holiday next month.

f We normally ask for a letter from your parents, but .... we'll make an exception.

g They've spent all their money and .... they are not going shopping tomorrow.

h They love trying out different restaurants, ... the new ones in town.

5 Complete the sentences using *except* or *accept*.

a They want us to .... the invitation to the party in writing.

b The staff will .... the wage rise but they want it from this month.

c You can choose what you want, ... the most expensive items.

d I .... your excuse but nonetheless you should not take time off school.

e We can go any day, ... the ones where the film starts very early.

f If you .... the gift, ... the money, then I think that would be a better idea.

g He never calls me, ... to borrow money.

h I immediately .... the position offered to me at the university.

B Language focus: phrases for giving advice

1 Look at the following sentences. Underline the advice phrases.

a If I were you, I'd visit the doctor soon to check that cough.

b I think it would be better if you came later, as I won't be ready.

c It might be a good idea to read the book before seeing the film.

d Why don't we take the dog for a walk now, before it rains?

e I don't think she should buy that car, as it's too expensive.

2 Which expressions in Exercise B1 are followed by *to*? Circle them. Which expressions are followed by an infinitive without *to*? Double underline them.

3 Below is a mixed-up dialogue. Put it in the correct order.

a **Merlin:** Yes, I think it would be better to go in the summer, as it'll be freezing now.

b **Merlin:** Are you coming on the school trip next week?

c **Merlin:** Yes, we could and I think you should tell them, as they like you …

d **Merlin:** Um … I don't think you should, as they're always rushing around at that time.

e **Merlin:** Yes, that's not a bad idea, and I think we should tell them soon.

f **Yvonne:** Yes, I'm thinking about it, but it's in the mountains and will be cold.

g **Yvonne:** Alright. Let's tell them during the break then?

h **Yvonne:** If I were you, I'd tell them tomorrow morning before classes start.

i **Yvonne:** Why don't we tell the teachers that?

1 b   2 ___   3 ___   4 ___   5 ___   6 ___   7 ___   8 ___   9 ___

4 Look at each of the following situations. Imagine you are talking to a friend and give them a piece of advice and a suggestion for each one.

Example: They have got a bad headache.
You should go and lie in a dark room.
You could take a painkiller.

a They are panicking before an exam.

....

....

b They've had a bad argument with their parents.

....

....

c They found a sick animal on the roadside.

....

....

d They haven't got enough money to go out.

....

....

C Skills

Reading and writing

1 a You are going to read about a television programme called *Dirty Jobs*. What do you think the programme is about? Tick those you think are correct.

i They are jobs which are only outside.

ii They are normally jobs that other people do not want to do.

iii People get their clothes and bodies dirty.

iv They are jobs which are normally only found in certain countries.

b List **three** dirty jobs that you would not like to do.

....

....

....

2 Skim the text *Dirty Jobs* and find words that have similar meanings to the words and phrases below.

a presenter (paragraph 1) ....

b jobs (1) ....

c with (1) ....

d test (1) ....

e combination (2) ....

f humour (2) ....

g dangers (3) ....

h result of (4) ....

i very visual (4) ....

j received large numbers of (4) ....

k paid for (4) ....

l idea (4) ....

m credit (4) ....

Dirty Jobs

[1] *Dirty Jobs* is a programme on the Discovery Channel in which the host, Mike Rowe, is shown performing difficult, strange and/or messy occupational duties alongside the typical employees. The show started with three pilot episodes in November 2003, and continued until 12 September 2012 with a total of 169 episodes and was shown and filmed all over the world including in Australia and Europe.

[2] The appeal of the show is the juxtaposition of Mike Rowe, a well-spoken man of television with a sharp, sarcastic wit, the situations in which he's put and the colourful personalities of the men and women who actually do that job for a living.

[3] A worker takes on Rowe as a fully involved assistant during a typical day at work, during which he works hard to complete every task as best he can despite discomfort, hazards or situations that are just plain disgusting. The 'dirty job' often includes the cameraman and rest of the crew getting just as dirty as Rowe. Nearly every job is even more difficult than he had expected, and this often has him expressing admiration and respect for the workers' skills and their willingness to take on jobs that most people avoid. The show always begins with the following quote from Rowe, usually spoken while in the midst of a particularly dirty task:

'My name's Mike Rowe, and this is my job. I explore the country looking for people who aren't afraid to get dirty – hard-working men and women who earn an honest living doing the kinds of jobs that make civilised life possible for the rest of us. Now, get ready to get dirty.'

[4] The show is a spin-off from a local San Francisco programme called *Somebody's Gotta Do It* that host Mike Rowe once did. After completing a graphic piece on cows and dairy farming, Rowe was inundated with letters expressing 'shock, horror, fascination, disbelief and wonder'. Rowe then sent the tape to the Discovery Channel, which commissioned a series based on this concept. Mike stated that he originally wanted to honour his father, a lifetime animal farmer, by bringing fame to the less-than-glorious careers.

3 Read the text in more detail, then complete the notes below.

Programme name **(a)** .... on **(b)** .... Channel. Show started in **(c)** .... with **(d)** .... episodes and ended in **(e)** .... Three things that are appealing about the show: the presenter, **(f)** .... and the **(g)** ....

Those getting dirty include Rowe, **(h)** .... and **(i)** .... Rowe works alongside other workers doing things that are uncomfortable, **(j)** .... or **(k)** .... Mike expresses his **(l)** .... and **(m)** .... for the people that do the dirty jobs because nobody else ever wants to do them. Also, it reminds him of the life his **(n)** .... led as an animal farmer which was also a dirty job. Originally, show called **(o)** ....

4 You are going to give a talk about Mike Rowe's programme to your class. Prepare some notes to use as the basis for your talk. Make short notes under each heading.

Details of the programme

- ....
- ....

Reasons for its appeal

- ....
- ....
- ....

Things that happen in the programme

- ....
- ....
- ....

Origins of the show

- ....
- ....

D Writing

1 Look at the advert below for the job of airport baggage handler. List three things that you think a baggage handler has to do and three things that you think make it a 'dirty job'.

Baggage handler tasks	What makes it a dirty job?

WANTED

Part-time airport baggage handlers (three needed)

Location:	Airport Terminal 1
Salary:	\$10–\$17 per hour, depending on shift hours, experience and age
Start date:	31 May
Job type:	Part-time, temporary
Hours:	10–15 hours per week, including weekends and nights (suitable for students)
Requirements:	Applicants need to be fit and healthy, as the position involves lifting and carrying. No formal academic qualifications are required, although preference is given to applicants with IGCSE English and Maths.

Note: As the job involves working outside in all weathers, a uniform is provided.

We are now recruiting baggage handlers for Terminal 1. This is a part-time, temporary position and shifts will range from 10 to 15 hours per week, depending on flight schedules. There are overtime opportunities when flight schedules increase. The job duties will include loading and offloading baggage to/from aircraft, and moving baggage to airport carousels for passengers to collect.

2 Imagine your friend is interested in applying for the job of baggage handler. Write a summary of the job description in your own words as far as possible.

You will receive up to 6 (Core) / 8 (Extended) marks for the content of your summary and up to 6 (Core) / 8 (Extended) marks for the style and accuracy of your language.

Your summary should be about 80 (Core) or 100 words long (Extended). You should use your own words as far as possible.

....

....

....

....

....

....

....

....

....

....

....

....

Unit 8

Communication

A Vocabulary

1 Match the words of the following numbers to those in the box.

1/5	63 064	314 000%	13th	10	492	100s	1 000 000	13–19	680

a hundreds ....

b one-fifth ....

c six hundred and eighty ....

d three hundred and fourteen thousand per cent ....

e thirteenth ....

f thirteen to nineteen ....

g one million ....

h four hundred and ninety-two ....

i sixty-three thousand and sixty-four ....

j ten ....

2 Now use the numbers in the box to complete the information.

a Jumbo jets use .... gallons of fuel to take off.

b The .... can be the luckiest or unluckiest number depending on where you live in the world.

c The average person eats almost .... kilograms of food a year.

d It takes .... seconds for sunlight to reach the Earth.

e There are .... ants for every person in the world.

f The annual growth of internet traffic is ....

g .... of all cancers are sun-related.

h Over the last 150 years, the average height of people in industrialised nations has increased by .... centimetres.

i The .... are also known as the 2nd century.

j .... year olds can be referred to as teenagers.

3 Match the American English word with the British English equivalent.

American English		British English	
faucet	trashcan	tap	dustbin
check	sidewalk	pavement	CV
janitor	truck	caretaker	lorry
diaper	restroom	nappy	bathroom
license plate	fall	autumn	postcode
résumé	cookie	number plate	biscuit
zucchini	gas	bill (restaurant)	courgette
zip code		petrol	

4 Choose **either** British English **or** American English. Then select words from your chosen list above to complete these sentences.

a Cars need to have a .... so that they can be identified by the police and their owner.

b It's best if your .... is short and to the point rather than a lot of unnecessary information.

c When you shop online, you always have to add your .... to complete the address.

d I think .... is the best season as the leaves look beautiful.

e I couldn't have a hot bath because the .... had got stuck and there was only cold water.

f I think .... cooked with egg is a very simple but tasty meal.

B Language focus: the passive

1 Look at these phrases with verbs in the passive

... school coursework would not be completed

Rome is documented ...

Decide if the following information is true or false

a The passive is formed with the verb *to be* + past participle. True / False

b *Am*, *is* and *are* are forms of the verb *to be*. True / False

c The passive voice focuses more on the action of a sentence. True / False

d The passive can only be formed in the past simple tense. True / False

e The passive is often used in formal and technical English. True / False

f In the passive, it is not always necessary to know who does the action. True / False

g There are no irregular verb forms in the past participle. True / False

2 Look at the following sentences which describe the history of communication. Underline all the examples of the use of the passive.

a The world's first known printed book is developed.

b The first demonstration of an electric telegraph is given by the US inventor Morse.

c The first personal computer known as 'Apple' is designed.

d Homing pigeons are used as postmen in Baghdad.

e A kind of paper made from bamboo is developed by the Chinese.

f The first postage stamp is introduced in Britain, called the Penny Black.

g The telephone is invented by an Italian called Marconi.

h The use of the first television is demonstrated in London.

i Writing is developed on clay tablets by the Sumerians.

3 Change the following sentences into the passive.

Example: People expect him to be the next Head of Science.
He is expected to be the next Head of Science.

a Firemen have reported that the fire is out of control.

....

b Some people think that saving money is better than spending it.

....

c The municipality built that ugly modern building and it cost hundreds of thousands of euros.

....

d Countries around the world celebrate different public holidays.

....

e NASA has sent up another satellite for the weather.

....

f People who loved the book *The Lord of the Rings* also enjoyed the film.

....

4 Rewrite the sentences in Exercise B2 in the year/era you think it happened below but changing the passive verb into past simple passive.

a 3100 BC ... Writing <u>was developed</u> on clay tablets by the Sumerians.

b 1500 BC ... .

c 865 ... .

d 1050 ... .

e 1838 ... .

f 1840 ... .

g 1871 ... .

h 1926 ... .

i 1976 ... .

C Skills

Reading

1 You are going to read an article about a parent's negative perspective on the effect the internet has on young people. Look at the following words from the article, then match each one with a definition from the box.

left alone very interested in twelve leading to success never ending excellent controlled or influenced being alone

a abandoned ....

b engrossed ....

c manipulated ....

d relentlessly ....

e dozen ....

f potential ....

g solitude ....

h exemplary ....

2 Before you read the article, look at the three statements below. Decide if they are true or false. Give a reason for your answers.

a The writer rarely sees a teenager without a computer or smartphone.
True / False ....

b The writer found that teenagers are always positive about their phones.
True / False ....

c Technology has taken the role of the parent.
True / False ....

3 Read the article and complete with words from Exercise C1. Then check if your answers to Exercise C2 were correct.

Have we abandoned ourselves and our children to the internet?

A year ago, I walked into my kitchen to find half a **(a)** .... teenagers there, each one **(b)** .... with their own private screen, in silence. I realised it had been months since I'd seen a teenager without a computer or smartphone in their hand.

But what surprised me was the anger of many teenagers who, in turn, felt **(c)** .... by parents whose own eyes were fixed on electronic devices. As, let's be honest with ourselves, it's not only young people who are at fault here.

The more I walked around and saw people around me, the more I realised how much of our lives are now spent communicating, not necessarily with the people we are physically with, but with the device that has become an invaluable part of our lives. We cannot do an activity any more without consulting, at some point, an electrical device. Have a look around you the next time you go to an event – whether it be a football match, a performance at the theatre or the cinema – how many people are using their phones to text, to use as a clock, to take a photo, etc.

Asking a young person, or anybody for that matter, to put down their Xbox, switch off their computer or stop looking at their smartphone is like asking a baby to put down its teddy bear. Behind the nursery colours and baby names is a culture that is **(d)** .... commercial. Each interaction means data – data that is worth a fortune. Both our children and ourselves are being **(e)** .... to become **(f)** .... consumers and we can increasingly admit we do not feel 'in control' of our own internet use. No site, or activity on the internet, is without the 'Permission cookie bar' appearing during use. As if we really have to have our permission asked in order for them to display some form of advertising; because it always appears, whether we want it or not.

I am still cautiously hopeful about the **(g)** .... of the internet. But it seems that the greatest revolution in communication has been hijacked by commercial values.

Becoming an adult human requires imitation and role models, it takes patience and practice, and it needs both **(h)** .... and community. Instead, many of our children have smartphones in the hands that we adults should be holding.

Adapted from: www.theguardian.com

4 Answer the following questions based on the article.

a In what way did the writer find the young people not communicating?

....

b How are young people reflecting what their carers do?

....

c Give **two** examples of how computers and smartphones appeal to young people.

....

d What happens each time a person goes online?

....

e What does the writer say has become the dominant feature of the internet?

....

f How has a computer taken the role of a parent?

....

D Writing

1 You have read an article in your school magazine about how young people feel their methods of communication differ from those of their parents. Here are some comments made in the article:

- I could not imagine life without a mobile phone even if it's just for letting my parents know where I am.
- I never phone my friends – we always message or text, but my parents always call me.
- I think my generation speaks less and communicates more with technology (Core only).
- I think my parents missed out on so much because they didn't have mobile phones and computers (Core only).

Write a letter to the school magazine editor giving your views on the subject.

The comments above may give you some ideas, but you should try to use some ideas of your own.

Your letter should be between 100/150 (Core) and 150/200 words long (Extended).

You will receive up to 7 (Core) / 10 (Extended) marks for the content of your letter and up to 7 (Core) / 10 (Extended) marks for the language.

....

....

....

....

....

....

....

....

....

....

....

....

Interviews

A Vocabulary

1 Some word forms can have two meanings. Find the word for each of the following. Sometimes the pronunciation of the word changes.

Example: A place where one can live F L A T Have a level surface

- **a** A fruit from a palm tree _ _ _ _ Day and month of the year
- **b** Worn on the arm for time _ _ _ _ _ To observe
- **c** Watches a game to check rules _ _ _ _ _ _ _ Confirms the character of a person
- **d** A command or instruction _ _ _ _ _ An arrangement or pattern
- **e** To indicate with the finger _ _ _ _ _ The sharp end of a pencil
- **f** A supporter _ _ _ Moves air to cool
- **g** Go away from _ _ _ _ _ Time away from school or work
- **h** To highlight an idea or sound _ _ _ _ _ _ Tension or worry
- **i** A sign or advertisement _ _ _ _ _ _ To observe or pay attention to
- **j** The bill in AmEng _ _ _ _ _ To make sure that something is right
- **k** To not allow or say 'no' _ _ _ _ _ _ Rubbish
- **l** Tiny or very small _ _ _ _ _ _ 60 seconds
- **m** To hit forcibly and deliberately _ _ _ _ _ _ An organised refusal to work

2 Choose the correct word in each of the following sentences.

- **a** It's not her **fault / drawback** that they arrived late as her car broke down.
- **b** The **fault / drawback** to this idea is that not everybody speaks the same language.
- **c** She has her **faults / drawbacks**, I suppose, but on the whole, she's a nice person.
- **d** There are so many **faults / drawbacks** to this holiday; like the cost, the place and the long flight.
- **e** The only **fault / drawback** with this accommodation is that it is so far from the bus stop.
- **f** A mechanical **fault / drawback** caused the car to come off the road and hit the traffic lights.

3 In Unit 9, you saw words ending with *-er* and *-ee*. Fill in the table below with similar words.

Doer	Recipient
	employee
interviewer	
	trainee
payer	
nominator	
	advisee

4 Use the correct form of the word from Exercise A3 to complete the following sentences.

a Each .... has been allocated 10 new ...., who they will shadow for the whole course.

b The .... sat nervously, waiting to be called in by the .... to find out about the job.

c On a cheque, you should clearly write the name of the .... on the top line.

d Our .... has requested that all staff arrive early tomorrow as we have a meeting about our salaries.

e You are not the only .... for the award, as there are 12 others.

f The former .... to the President has been fired due to misconduct in office.

5 Choose the word which best completes the sentence.

a A .... sent to an employer should be professional, but short and informative.

CV	biography	summary	review

b You don't need many educational .... for this job as they are interested in a person's background more.

experience	skills	qualifications	competence

c I'm interested in this job. The .... is on Monday morning.

conversation	meeting	dialogue	interview

d The company has called the people whose names I gave as ....

referees	judges	officials	umpires

e You need a specific .... for this position and I don't think I qualify.

intelligence	expertise	skill	job

f The level of .... at the various schools in the area is extremely varied and shows in their examination results.

study	training	learning	education

g You should write your full .... in capital letters and in black ink.

surname	name	brand	signature

h You should list your .... on your application as employers like to see you as a person.

amusement	sport	hobbies	occupation

B Language focus: the imperative

1 Complete the table by matching the function of the imperative form with its example. Then write your own example.

Functions: ~~A direct order~~ / To give instructions / To make an invitation / On a sign or notice / To give friendly formal advice / Make an offer / Give a warning

Example: Come for dinner / Keep out! / Have a quiet word with her about it / Turn the pages slowly / Hello. Have a seat / Come here! / Careful

Function	Example	Your example
A direct order		

2 Andreas is going for an interview and his mother is helping him to get ready. Complete the sentences with the words from the box.

be polite	make sure	be smart	accept	don't shake	
try	take	be careful	don't wear	tidy up	look interested

a .... that yellow tie with that green shirt – it's horrible.

b .... and have your clothes ready the night before.

c .... hands unless their hand is offered first.

d .... not to look too nervous.

e .... and look people in the eye when you talk to them.

f .... how you sit in the interview room and certainly sit up straight.

g .... you arrive early at the place and .... your clothes and hair before you introduce yourself to the receptionist.

h .... a copy of the job description and the questions that you want to ask the interviewers.

i .... and respectful towards everyone.

j .... a drink if it's offered to you, but drink quietly.

3 Now imagine you are helping your friend complete an application form for a job as a sales assistant in a shop. Use the following structures to give him some advice.

a Don't ....

b Thank ....

c Do ....

d Read ....

e Write ....

f Complete ....

C Skills

Listening

1 **CD 2, Track 20** You will hear six people talking about their experience of university interviews. For each of Speakers 1–6, choose from the list, A to G, which opinion each speaker expresses. Write the speaker's number next to the statement. Use each statement only once. There is one extra statement which you do not need to use.

A Behaving well is very important in an interview.

B I get nervous about all types of interviews.

C It's important to be prepared before the interview.

D I feel disadvantaged in a group.

E I need to think of what I am doing in an interview.

F Being prepared is one of my strong points.

G I always worry when I'm in front of a camera.

D Writing

1 In Unit 9, Exercise D3 of your Coursebook, you created your own CV. Your teacher now wants you to use the information in your CV to write a description of yourself. Write three paragraphs, as follows:

- Paragraph 1: Personal details, and education and qualifications
- Paragraph 2: Work experience, and hobbies and interests
- Paragraph 3: Other skills

Write 40–50 words for each paragraph.

Education

A Vocabulary

1 Make words using the letters in the boxes to complete the gaps.

ate	am	act	tech	on	on	or	~~me~~	to	elm
on	in	and	ate	are	on	cat	an	port	

concentr......

prep......

ign......e

sup......

underst......

ex......ination

ho<u>me</u>work

......nique

dedi......ed

overwh......ing

dim......ishes

recogniti......

recollecti......

retenti......

inter......

c......cept

formul......

......pic

cosmopolit......

2 Complete the sentences below with words from Exercise A1.

Example: Our teacher gave us so much <u>homework</u> this weekend.

- **a** They are great friends and are very .... to each other.
- **b** The pain .... with time as the bones mend and get stronger.
- **c** There is a certain .... in how you should lift heavy things.
- **d** He has no .... of what happened after the accident.
- **e** The trainees get a lot of .... during the initial stages of the course.
- **f** You need to .... much more when you drive to avoid accidents.
- **g** The amount of support for the refugees was so ...., that I cried.
- **h** The students need to .... much more with each other.
- **i** London is a very .... city and many different nationalities live there.

3 Complete the sentences with the correct form of *engage* or *concentrate*.

- **a** The children need to be much more .... with the activities in the class.
- **b** .... on the picture for two minutes and your eyes will feel strange.
- **c** She has been .... by the new company that has set up offices here.
- **d** I think you should .... on your work for now and forget about going to the gym.
- **e** She couldn't .... on the film and so decided to leave early and go home.
- **f** The tasks must .... the children or they will quickly get bored.

4 Complete the crossword.

Across

3 Time given to learning (5)

7 Method used to assess level (11)

8 Educational talk (7)

10 Extra work given by the teacher (8)

Down

1 Higher place of learning (7)

2 The process of learning (9)

4 Clothes worn in school (7)

5 Place of learning (6)

6 Person who gives the learning (7)

9 Brief record of ideas (5)

B Language focus: alternative conditional structures

1 Look at the following sentences. What structures or tenses are the underlined verbs?

a If you make so many cakes, take one for yourself. ....

b You might want to go earlier if you're worried about the buses. ....

c If you go earlier, you will get your choice of seat. ....

d If you buy the tickets now, you are saving a lot of money. ....

e When you're training so hard every day, you can get dehydrated. ....

f Don't stand up if you have a seat! ....

2 Match each example (a–f) in Exercise B1 with one of the following combinations (i–vi):

i imperative/present simple

ii modal + infinitive/present simple

iii present continuous/modal + infinitive

iv present simple/imperative

v present simple/present continuous

vi present simple/future

3 Complete the conditional sentence by putting the tense into the correct form.

a If they **(have)** .... time during the week, they'll go to the cinema on Saturday.

b If we leave quietly now, nobody **(notice)** ....

c If we **(know)** .... about your money issues, we would've helped you.

d If I **(be)** .... you, I would not buy those green trousers.

e We **(arrive)** .... earlier if we had not missed the train.

f If I didn't have a mobile phone, my life **(not be)** .... the same.

g That's no problem; I **(get)** .... the food if you buy the drinks.

h If I **(tell)** .... you something, you would be sure not to tell anybody.

i She **(go)** .... out with you if you had invited her along.

j I wouldn't have read your notes, if you **(not hide)** .... them in such an obvious place.

4 Complete these sentences with information about yourself.

a If it rains tonight, ...

b If I'd been born 100 years ago, ...

c If I don't pass my end-of-year exams, ...

d If I could stop time, ...

e If I were a fish, ...

C Skills

Reading

1 The following words and phrases appear in the text below. Match them to the correct definition. Use a dictionary to help you understand any unknown words.

contribute	short	salary	graduate	academic
reputation	initially	depend	expenses	

a connected to education ....

b money you earn ....

c not enough ....

d costs ....

e to begin with ....

f add ....

g good name ....

h person who has a university degree ....

i rely ....

2 The title of the text is 'I was concerned I would be left out'. What do you think the speaker meant by 'left out'?

a on my own

b left alone

c not included

3 Skim the text and check whether your answer to Exercise C2 is correct.

I was concerned I would be left out

Bimla knew that she wanted to go to university when she got her IGCSE results. But she had been worried that she would not be accepted by the other students once she got there.

Although she had always been told at her school that she would do well at university, she nonetheless believed that other students would be better than her. 'I know I got good grades at school, but I thought that they wouldn't be enough and that I would be left out by the other students,' she admits. Some of her friends thought she shouldn't even think about going to university, but she didn't agree with that and said, 'I think university should be for everyone, no matter where they come from or what their background is.'

Growing up in a large family, she'd always understood that her parents would depend on the children to contribute money to the home. 'We all knew we'd have to help pay the expenses at home, so when I told my parents I wanted to do my IGCSEs before going to university, they weren't very pleased initially,' she recalls. 'But soon they accepted the idea when they thought about the advantages of having a university graduate in the family.'

Money was short at home, so Bimla worked after her IGCSEs and saved nearly everything from her salary. She wanted to work in medicine, so she looked around and found a university near home, which meant she could stay at home and study at the same time. It wasn't easy travelling to and from university each day but she would find that she could use the time sitting on the train in a constructive way. She had her favourite seat and would make a beeline for it when she got on. She would then know that she had a good hour in which she could do some real studying, and since most people on the train were adults going to work, then the atmosphere tended to be subdued. So with her studying, travelling and going to work, she found that she had little time to socialise. But that wasn't a priority for her because she knew that she wasn't the only one making sacrifices for her studying, particularly when she saw her parents working all hours to provide for the family and knew that they were also doing this to support her in the best way they knew.

The university had a good academic reputation and she thought she wouldn't get in, so she was very excited when she was offered a place. 'I never thought it possible,' she admits.

Three years later and she remembers her fears of being left out. 'I've made some really great friends and everybody has been so helpful, even the lecturers! The idea that you are not good enough because you are different is so wrong – university is not like that.'

She wants to say to other families, 'If your child is good enough and really wants to go on to university, then you can't imagine the advantages there will be for you and your family.'

4 Find and underline the vocabulary from Exercise C1 in the text.

5 Now say if the following are true or false.

a	Bimla wanted to go to university because of her friends.	True / False
b	She thought she was as good as the other students.	True / False
c	Bimla believed that university should be open to all types of people.	True / False
d	Bimla's parents expected all their children to go to work after school.	True / False
e	Bimla was the first person in her family to go to university.	True / False
f	She had to study on the train as there was no room at home.	True / False
g	The university she applied to had high standards.	True / False
h	People have not been friendly towards her at university because she's different.	True / False

D Speaking

1 Imagine you are sitting in an exam and you have been given 2–3 minutes to study the topic card and prepare. Look at the following topics from the Coursebook and for each one write as many notes as you can in those 2–3 minutes.

- Studying abroad
- Education as a preparation for work

Write some notes:

....

....

....

....

....

....

....

....

....

....

....

....

Unit 11
Achievements

A Vocabulary

1 Read the clues and complete the words. The first and last letter of each word is given to help you.

a	a _ _ _ _ _ _ _ _ _ t	A thing done successfully with effort.
b	b _ _ _ _ t	A type of dance.
c	e _ _ _ _ _ _ _ t	The necessary items for a particular purpose.
d	e _ _ _ t	A thing that happens or takes place.
e	r _ _ _ _ d	The summary of past achievements or performance.
f	p _ _ _ _ _ t	Keep something from happening.
g	c _ _ _ _ _ t	Bring or gather something together.
h	s _ _ _ _ _ _ _ t	Most unusual.
i	m _ _ _ _ _ _ _ _ _ a	Objects kept or collected because of an association.
j	w _ _ _ _ _ g s _ _ _ k	A support for walking.

2 Choose words from the box which are similar in meaning to the given words/phrases in bold.

irresponsible	rations	stumbled	struggled	explorer	
~~achievement~~	blizzard	legible	alternative	inhalation	dissuade

Example: Many people question that Robert Scott made any great *accomplishment*.

a You should **try to stop** the children from crossing the road alone. ....

b Robert Scott was if anything a great **adventurer** for his time. ....

c They died from the **breathing in** of smoke from the raging fire. ....

d I think if you take a **different** route to school, you should get there quicker. ....

e He has been very **childish** in his attitude towards learning to drive. ....

f A great **storm** raged and prevented people getting out doing things. ....

g He hit his head on the window and **fell** into the room in a stupor. ....

h He had beautiful **clear** handwriting which he took great pride in. ....

i Everybody was given equal **supplies**, which had to be carried individually. ....

j They **tried hard** to reach their goal but were beaten by another team. ....

3 Write the digits for the following numbers.

Example: twenty-one = 21

a sixty-two point seventy-one kilograms ....

b one hundred and twenty-three ....

c sixty thousand ....

d fifty-six point seven degrees centigrade ....

e five point seventy-eight seconds ....

f fourteen thousand four hundred and ten ....

g twenty-three thousand four hundred and ten ....

h thirty-three thousand three hundred and thirty-three ....

4 Facts and figures from around the world. Use the numbers from the box to complete the information.

$21 787 000	162 minutes	56.3%	8 hours and 50 minutes
157 348 000	150 million	$150 000	8.1
86.2	1 166 000 tonnes		

a The French sleep more than any other country, sleeping about .... a day.

b China produces the most tea in the world at ....

c The US is the largest donor of aid to other countries, giving ....

d Japanese women live the longest, with the average at .... years.

e The distance of Earth from the Sun is about .... kilometres.

f Greeks are the biggest smokers, smoking on average .... cigarettes a day.

g Today the US has the most Facebook users with numbers at .... but this is expected to fall.

h Turks spend the most time eating and drinking, on average .... per day.

i The most expensive office space is found in Hong Kong at .... per square foot.

j Rwanda has the highest number of female Members of Parliament with .... of seats.

5 When you have completed the sentences read them out loud, saying the numbers correctly.

B Language focus: superlatives, past perfect

1 Respond to the following situations. Use the prompts and a superlative in each of your responses.

Example: You've just had a very boring lesson. ***(boring/lesson/attend)***
<u>That was the most boring lesson I've ever attended.</u>

a You've just seen a film which you found very sad. **(sad/film/see)**

....

b You're in Dubai, looking at the Burj Khalifa building. **(tall/building/world?)**

....

c You're looking at a picture of the animal the cheetah. **(fast/animal/world)**

....

d You've been running a long distance with your friend. **(far/run)**

....

e You're looking at two dresses and neither has a price tag. **(expensive?)**

....

f You've been trying different teas and say which you prefer. **(English breakfast/tasty)**

....

g You've been shopping and have heavy bags. Ask your brother to take one. **(carry/heavy/bag?)**

....

h You're talking about paintings at a gallery and stating your preference. **(beautiful)**

....

2 Put the verbs into the past perfect simple tense.

Example: My phone didn't work because I'd forgotten the charger. ***(forget)***

a When she went out to the cinema, she .... her homework. **(already/do)**

b The cat ate all the chicken that my mum .... **(just/cook)**

c He .... to the countryside before last year. **(not/be)**

d When she arrived at the theatre, the play .... **(already/start)**

e They .... in Italy before they moved to France for good. **(live)**

f If you .... to me, you would have got that job. **(listen)**

g My brother .... home by the time I arrived. **(get)**

h She got really upset when she realised she .... her laptop on the bus. **(leave)**

i The children were really hungry because they .... for ages. **(not eat)**

j The children .... their teacher's birthday and bought her flowers. **(not/forget)**

3 **a** Look at the words *kilometre* and *kilometres* in this sentence.
Men compete in 20 kilometre and 50 kilometre races; women only race 20 kilometres.
What part of speech is each word? ....

b Complete the following sentences using an appropriate phrase from the box. Is each phrase an adjective or a noun?

16 years old	50-dollar	50-gram	500 dollars	500 grams	one-thousand-year-old

i The box of chocolates weighed ...., but most of that was packaging.

ii It was a .... building.

iii The watch cost more than ...., and it's made of platinum.

iv That's a .... piece of gold, but I have no idea of its value.

v He's only ...., but he's already got a place in the first team.

vi It was only a .... ticket, but the service was excellent.

C Skills

Reading

1 Look at the names of the people below. Do you know any of the names or why the people are famous for their achievements? Match the names with their area of interest.

a	Jean-Francois Champollion	**i**	Campaigns for girls' education
b	Wolfgang Amadeus Mozart	**ii**	Linguist
c	Nadia Comaneci	**iii**	Author
d	Malala Yousafzai	**iv**	Developed reading system for the blind
e	Mary Shelley	**v**	Olympic gymnast
f	Louis Braille	**vi**	Pioneer and nurse
g	J.R.R. Tolkien	**vii**	Author
h	Florence Nightingale	**viii**	Composed classical music

2 Write the name of the person you would like to know more about. Explain why.

....

3 Name a person who you think has made a great achievement.

....

4 Give three reasons why you think their achievement is great.

a ....

b ....

c ....

5 Check your answers to Exercise C1 by reading the text and underlining one word that helped you find the correct answer.

Which person …?

Certain people's names have become synonymous with certain events in life and will always be names that people recognise. People, young and old, will always recognise famous and infamous names and be able to associate them with achievements, however much they might question their success. The names below are from various eras, ages and backgrounds, and their achievements vary just as much.

Jean-Francois Champollion was born in France in 1790. He displayed a natural talent for languages from an early age and by his mid-teens he had mastered Latin, Greek, Arabic, Hebrew and Sanskrit. If it hadn't been for his love and awareness of language, we wouldn't today have seen that the symbols used in Egyptian hieroglyphics are actually a mix of pictographics and alphabetical letters. This breakthrough has enabled others to crack the code of a long-lost language.

Wolfgang Amadeus Mozart lived from 1756 to 1791 and was a composer born in Salzburg, Austria. He was initially taught by his father but as he grew older he showed prodigious ability and from the age of five had composed his first works and performed in front of European royalty. During Mozart's short life he wrote more than forty symphonies, twenty-two operas and many other works. Today he remains among the most enduringly popular of classical composers, and his influence has been profound on subsequent Western music.

Nadia Comaneci was born in 1961 in Romania where she started gymnastics from kindergarten age. She was only 14 years old when she received the first 'perfect 10' score in gymnastics and in the 1976 Olympics, held in Montreal, Canada, she won three gold medals. She went on to win two more gold medals in the 1980 Olympics in Moscow and is one of the best-known gymnasts in the world.

Malala Yousafzai was born in July 1997 and is a Pakistani blogger and child rights activist who is committed to maintaining the right of education for girls. In October 2012 she was shot on her way home from school by those opposed to her ideas. Her achievements have included being awarded the Nobel Peace Prize in 2014, being voted one of the most influential people in the world and speaking at the United Nations headquarters to talk about access to education for all.

Mary Shelley lived from 1797 to 1851 and was a British writer. She is best known for her novel *Frankenstein*, which marked the beginning of two entire genres of fiction, horror and science fiction. Shelley authored the classic novel when she was nineteen years old and it remains widely read and has inspired many theatrical and film adaptations. It was published anonymously in 1818 because during that period it was not seen as appropriate that a woman should be an author, particularly considering the theme of the book.

Louis Braille lived from 1809 to 1852 and was a French educator and inventor of a system of reading and writing for use by the blind or visually impaired. His system remains known worldwide simply as braille. Blinded in both eyes as a result of an early childhood accident, Braille mastered his disability while still a boy. He excelled in his education and when still a student began developing a system of tactile code that could allow blind people to read and write quickly and efficiently.

John Ronald Reuel Tolkien lived from 1892 to 1973 and was an English writer, philologist and university professor, best known as the author of several influential fantasy books such as *The Hobbit* and *The Lord of the Rings*. He had a lifelong interest in and love of language, and also created several constructed languages. He has popularly been identified as the 'father' of modern fantasy literature and in 2008, he was ranked sixth on a list of 'The 50 greatest British writers since 1945'.

Florence Nightingale lived from 1820 to 1910 and was an English nurse during the Crimean War (1854–56) where she tended wounded soldiers. She was a pioneer of modern nursing and decisive in professionalising nursing roles for women. In 1860, Nightingale laid the foundation of professional nursing with the establishment of her nursing school at St Thomas' Hospital in London. It was the first secular nursing school in the world, now part of King's College London.

Adapted from*: *An article on www.conservapedia.com

6 For the following questions (a–j) about the text, choose one of the eight people in the text you read previously.

Which person …

a had to learn to read in a different way from other children? ....

b created new words and language systems? ....

c identified an old form of communication? ....

d continued her work after a personal tragedy? ....

e moved faultlessly? ....

f played in front of kings and queens? ....

g began developing a system of reading where blind people used their fingers?

....

h started a career for women? ....

i hid that she was female? ....

j had more than one job? ....

7 Look again at what the people above have achieved and select the person who you feel has made the greatest achievement.

Write a paragraph of about 80–100 words in which you give your reasons why. Write your introductory sentence in a similar style to the ones in the audioscript in the Coursebook: *I really think XXX made the greatest achievement*. Continue your paragraph, giving specific reasons for your opinion.

....

....

....

....

....

....

....

....

....

....

....

....

Unit 12
Organisations

A Vocabulary

1 Find the 12 words in the wordsearch. The words can be found in any direction.

adventure	continents	destination	emergencies	environment
expedition	exploration	hemisphere	location	organisation
programme	teenagers			

c	s	l	g	y	n	a	f	i	a	d	y	n	s	o
o	r	o	k	r	l	y	u	c	e	s	q	h	n	r
n	e	c	c	l	l	z	u	s	i	s	c	i	o	g
t	g	a	a	z	q	u	t	e	e	y	w	g	i	a
i	a	t	f	y	w	i	r	i	h	f	w	q	t	n
n	n	i	n	z	n	u	c	h	o	r	z	c	i	i
e	e	o	u	a	t	n	d	o	r	m	b	x	d	s
n	e	n	t	n	e	m	n	o	r	i	v	n	e	a
t	t	i	e	g	r	q	n	h	r	p	c	l	p	t
s	o	v	r	r	i	r	j	c	u	l	e	v	x	i
n	d	e	x	p	l	o	r	a	t	i	o	n	e	o
a	m	e	r	e	h	p	s	i	m	e	h	h	z	n
e	p	r	o	g	r	a	m	m	e	k	r	o	d	j
y	r	k	x	j	l	g	j	h	x	e	t	a	j	h
f	j	f	d	t	u	k	r	c	e	a	m	a	q	b

2 Use the words from Exercise A1 to complete the following sentences.

a Australia is in the southern .... and Switzerland is in the northern.

b In the world there are seven ...., and the largest is Asia.

c There are many different types of holiday you can go on, such as .... ones.

d There is a/an .... on Sunday to the mountains, to an area of great beauty.

e There has been so much .... recently that not much is untouched.

f The .... on the ticket would suggest that you're going the wrong way!

g .... have a hard time growing up these days, I think, with many challenges.

h The hospital has been busy this weekend with many ....

i The .... of the hotel is amazing!! You can see all of the bay.

j It was a very noisy .... during the exam and I could not concentrate.

k The new .... is to encourage young business people and will last for six months.

l They have set up a/an .... at school in which to help bullied children.

3 Complete the sentences using *location(s)* or *destination(s).*

a I really can't understand the .... of their house and need a map.

b The holiday home is in a great .... and right on the seafront.

c There are many different .... that you can choose from in the brochure.

d It doesn't say the .... on the ticket, so I don't know where we're going.

e Cyprus is a popular .... for tourists to visit in Europe.

f The movie was filmed in an amazing .... in New Zealand.

4 Find another shorter word within each word. Use the clues to help you.

Example: Population – make a loud explosive sound – pop

a Caribbean – a seed that you can eat ....

b archipelago – something that has a curved shape ....

c separated – consider to be of a certain quality or standard ....

d Antigua – a very small insect that lives under the ground ....

e questions – a long search for something ....

f organised – a large musical instrument normally found in a church ....

g knowledge – the present ....

h activity – behave in a specific way ....

i island – earth that is not covered by water ....

j hemisphere – a kind of ball shape ....

B Language focus: non-defining relative clauses, *either/or* and *neither/nor*

1 Complete the information about non-defining relative clauses using these words:

remove	someone	sentence	sense	extra information

Remember: A non-defining relative clause provides .... about .... or something. If we .... the non-defining relative clause from a ...., it will still make ....

2 Underline the clause if it can be omitted from the following sentences.

Example: We talked about our holiday, *which is arranged for next month*.

a They had to feed the poor cat, which stole the little boy's dinner.

b Do you still go to that restaurant, the one which we went to last year?

c There is the woman, who owns the bread shop, but she's obviously not working today.

d To get to Alberto's house, take the road that has lots of tall trees along it.

e The lady who lives next door has offered to look after my house while I'm away.

f Nektarios, who offered to lend me some money, is a great friend.

g I'm looking for the person whose car is blocking mine.

h He received very bad grades for his essays, which he finished quickly.

3 Combine the sentences by including an appropriate relative clause.

Example: Drinking plenty of water is a sensible thing to do. It keeps your body hydrated. Drinking plenty of water, which keeps your body hydrated, is a sensible thing to do.

a Keeping fit is a very important way to keep healthy. It should be done regularly.

....

b Michael went to university in London. He went to study English Literature.

....

c Michael had to leave the university. He was too poor to pay the fees.

....

d My grandmother is 75. She goes swimming every day in the lake.

....

e The car costs \$150 000. It can reach speeds of up to 300 kph.

....

f These trousers only cost me \$15. They are a lovely dark blue colour.

....

4 Look at the following sentences with *either/or*, *neither/nor* and correct where necessary.

a Neither Sara nor Emily do as they are told. ....

b Either the teacher or the secretary has the keys to the classroom. ....

c Either the dogs or the cat has to go. ....

d Hassan could not find the key neither on nor under the mat. ....

e She did not find her purse either on or under the sofa. ....

f He mentioned neither the test nor his result. ....

5 Complete these sentences using *either/or* or *neither/nor*.

a We can eat .... now .... later when he leaves to go to work, as the food is ready.

b You could ask them to come .... Monday .... Tuesday, I really don't mind as I'm not busy.

c .... my mother .... my father went to university and that's why they so much want me to go.

d She tried on both the dresses but .... the cheap one .... the expensive one looked nice on her.

e .... they tell us now if they're coming to the cinema .... I'm just going without them.

f .... the French .... the Italian teams were successful in getting to the finals.

C Skills

Reading

1 You are going to read some information about an organisation in Mexico that cares for endangered feline animals. Before you read the text, match the information and pictures.

a Oncilla ....

b Ocelot ....

c Jaguar ....

d Black panther ....

i One of the smallest cat species in the Americas, about 2.5 kg. These small-built and small-boned cats have a narrow head and white line above the eyes like make-up.

ii The name of any big cat with a black coat. These are mostly found as leopards in Asia and Africa, and jaguars in South America.

iii These are the largest felines in the Americas and live mostly in rainforests.

iv Twice the size of a house cat. They are mainly nocturnal and hunt rabbits, fish, frogs, etc.

2 Look at the information about the organisation's mission statement and match the headings in A with the information in B.

A	B
a Rescue	**i** To work with the authorities to keep changing laws in order to protect all species of animals.
b Raise awareness	**ii** As with our avian project, we aim to release the animals into the wild with the help of our supporters and the government.
c Mexican government	**iii** We aim to save many animals in need from sad circumstances, like circuses, captivity and pets.
d Endangered bird	**iv** To educate people worldwide about these animals and to learn to love and respect them and their environments.

3 Now read the text in more detail and answer the questions below.

About Us

The Black Jaguar-White Tiger™ Foundation is a non-profit organisation and it is about changing people's attitudes and perceptions about all animals. It is rooted in the belief that education can start a revolution; a revolution about love and respect for all living beings.

Who Are We?

The Foundation was inspired by a single unexpected act of love, and a whole lot of trust and magic.

Eduardo Serio, a Mexican-born businessman who was residing in Los Angeles, went on a business trip to Mexico, in 2013. While there, he received a call from his cousin, an animal expert with over 25 years of experience, who shared his frustration that a pet store was selling a baby Black Jaguar with the purpose of having it pose for photographs against its will and then using the money earned as a source of income.

Eduardo jumped at this opportunity and rescued Cielo from a life of captivity, leaving his whole life in L.A. behind. That single event gave birth to what today is The Black Jaguar-White Tiger™ Foundation.

Currently, with the help of devoted friends and millions of loyal followers around the world, the Foundation has rescued and cares for over 210 (and counting) big felines and more from an unhappy life in circuses, zoos and breeders, both legal and illegal. The Foundation has also rescued more than 20 street dogs.

The Foundation also has a project with the Mexican Government to reproduce, reintroduce and repopulate endangered species of birds, endemic to Mexico, into their natural habitat.

Their Mission has four main purposes:

1 To rescue many animals in need from sad circumstances such as circuses, breeding facilities and from people that have them as pets, providing them with a home, the best food and medical care available and a life of dignity and love for the rest of their lives.

2 To raise awareness worldwide through pictures, videos, using social media platforms and by giving conferences. To make the millions of people that follow them, fall in love with the rescued animals, so that as a consequence they learn to fall in love with their planet.

3 To continue working hand in hand with the Mexican Government, to keep changing laws in order to protect all species of animals in Mexico and inspire all countries around the world to join in.

4 As with the endangered bird project (reproduction and reintroduction into the wild), to work with the Mexican Government to start the same programme with feline species native to Mexico, like Jaguars, Ocelots and Oncillas.

There is the belief that in a couple of years, with all the support and awareness being raised, that the lost lion, tiger and leopard habitats in Africa and Asia will be regained, and perhaps help increase the numbers of these species.

Philosophy

To eventually release the animals, that have been cared for, into the wild from where they came and this option will impact upon our breeding programme. We have found that since the animals were born and currently live in captivity, they are happier in larger groups, regardless of the species. So there are prides that go from three individuals up to sixteen, and certain groups have members of different species but they nonetheless love and respect each other and live together harmoniously and it is this balance that we do not want to threaten.

***Adapted from*: blackjaguarwhitetiger.org**

a What is the aim of The Black Jaguar-White Tiger™ Foundation?

....

b Where was Eduardo when his cousin contacted him?

....

c Where are animals rescued from? Give **three** details.

....

....

....

d Other than felines, which other types of animal are helped?

....

e What does the Foundation eventually hope to do with all the animals? Give **four** details.

....

....

....

f What does the Mexican Government want to motivate other countries to do?

....

g What is the hope for the homes of felines in Africa and Asia?

....

h Under what circumstances will rescued animals be allowed to breed?

....

i What is the result of many animals living together?

....

4 Write answers for these questions:

a Do you like or dislike the Foundation described above? Why?

....

....

b Would you contribute money to the Foundation? If yes, why? If not, why not?

....

....

c Should people contribute money to foundations like this? Why/why not?

....

....

D Writing

Imagine that you won a school competition and have spent two days at the headquarters of The Black Jaguar-White Tiger™ Foundation. All your travel and hotel expenses were paid for.

Here are two comments from people you met during your visit

'Our daily work includes rescuing animals from many different difficult situations'

'We need a revolution to help people understand how to love and respect all living things'

Write a review of your visit explaining what you learned, and how you plan to pass on your experiences to your family and friends.

Your review should be between 150 and 200 words long.

The comments above may give you some ideas, and you can also use some ideas of your own.

You will receive up to 8 marks for the content of your review, and up to 8 marks for the language used.

....

....

....

....

....

....

....

....

....

....

....

....

Unit 13

Famous people

A Vocabulary

1 There are 12 nouns that describe a person's character in the word circle below, most of which come from Unit 13. Find and circle each of the nouns.

sociability confidencededicationdeterminationfearlessnessindependenceselfishnessskillstrengthambitionoptimismdominance

2 Write a noun from Exercise A1 next to its adjective synonym.

a self-assured ....

b loyal ....

c stubborn ....

d cheerful ....

e courageous ....

f self-reliant ....

g self-centred ....

h controlling ....

i experienced ....

j tough ....

k determined (to succeed) ....

l friendly ....

3 In the Coursebook you read about Bruce Lee. Which three of the adjectives in Exercise A2 do you think best describe his character?

a ....

b ....

c ....

4 Think of two other famous people and use three adjectives to describe their characters.

Name 1	Name 2 ....
....	....
....	....
....	....

5 Use reference sources to check the meaning of the following adjectives.

a ferocious

b bewildering

c prolific

d accessible

e renowned

6 Read the paragraph about the famous author, C.S. Lewis, and complete the gaps using the adjectives in Exercise A5.

A famous person I admire and who was a/an **(a)** .... writer, is C.S. Lewis. By the time of his death in 1963, he had written a/an **(b)** .... number of books concerning both fiction and fantasy. His books, and the style he wrote in, made them **(c)** .... to both adults and children. During his life-time, he became **(d)** .... in his opinion about struggles and sacrifices people are asked to make for their country. Today he is **(e)** .... mainly for the books that he wrote for children, which have since become successful films, namely: *The Chronicles of Narnia*.

7 Now write five sentences about a famous person you admire, using the words in Exercise A5.

a ....

b ....

c ....

d ....

e ....

8 Complete the sentences using *obstacle* or *problem*.

a There is a/an .... with the television: the volume has gone very quiet.

b The one big .... to her joining the police academy is that she is too short.

c There are a lot of .... on that road and quite a few accidents happen.

d Why do you create so many .... for her? You're holding her back.

e There was a/an .... with the transport this morning, so people were late.

f The .... to their buying the new car, is that they haven't got enough cash.

B Language focus: discourse markers, words ending in *-ly*

1 Connect the two sentences using the following discourse markers. You can use the same ones more than once. You may need to add some extra words to make meaningful sentences.

although	nonetheless	yet	the fact	on the other hand
still	even though	however	anyway	nevertheless

Example: The dress was very beautiful. She could not buy it.
<u>Although</u> the dress was very beautiful, she could not buy it.

a It is a really expensive holiday. They are going for a week.

....

b They were both invited to the exhibition. Only one of them is going.

....

c He was very careful with carrying the plates. He broke five of them.

....

d The book was really difficult to read. She finished it in a week.

....

e She had just eaten her dinner. She also ate a cake.

....

f She sat and revised for the test all night. She failed the exam.

....

g She has put on so much weight. She goes to the gym most days.

....

h The price for local apples has fallen. People are buying imported ones.

....

i She doesn't like cats very much. They've adopted two kittens.

....

2 Complete the sentences using the appropriate word. Say if the word chosen is an adverb, a noun, a verb or an adjective.

Example: He made the speech <u>briefly</u> because people wanted their dinner. ***Adverb***

aimlessly	architecturally	apply	supply	~~briefly~~	comply
difficulty	elderly	lively	nastily		

a The little boy was lost and walked .... through the streets.

b She had great .... learning the language and so decided to give it up.

c They had to .... with the rules of the school, as did all the students.

d She decided to .... for the education grant so that she could go to university.

e .... the building was beautiful, but it was totally impractical for families to live in.

f They were a very .... group of children and made a lot of noise.

g The .... of water to many parts of the country was made difficult by the weather.

h Seats should be offered to .... people on public transport.

i They gossiped .... about the new employee and made her first day unpleasant.

C Skills

Reading

1 Look at the pictures.

Who is this? LIFXE GRAEAURMNBT ....

What did he break? HET NSDUO RRREBIA ....

Unscramble the letters to find out.

2 Complete the sentence below using the words in the box, and find out why he is famous.

skydiver	sound barrier	capsule	space	helium balloon
Austrian	dangerous	extreme		

Felix Baumgartner is a/an **(a)** .... daredevil and **(b)** ...., who broke the **(c)** .... with an extremely **(d)** .... jump from **(e)** .... He first travelled to **(f)** .... heights in a **(g)** ...., which was towed by a huge **(h)** .... kilometres above Earth – and then he made the jump.

3 You are going to read about Felix Baumgartner. Before you read, look at the words and phrases from the text in the left-hand column and match them to their meaning.

a sound barrier	**i** The occurrence of two or more unplanned things at the same time.
b helium	**ii** Crying.
c capsule	**iii** A reckless and very daring person.
d daredevil	**iv** Pulled.
e towed	**v** An act or achievement that shows courage, strength or skill.
f freefall	**vi** To send something into outer space or the air.
g launch	**vii** A sudden increase in air resistance to something nearing the speed of sound.
h weeping	**viii** A gas that is lighter than air.
i famed	**ix** A small part of a spacecraft.
j incidents	**x** A fast or continuing drop.
k coincidentally	**xi** Famous, well known.
l feat	**xii** Events or occurrences.

4 Look at these six pieces of information. There is a mistake in each one. Quickly read the text to find and correct the mistakes.

Example: Swiss nationality. Austrian

a He fell from a height equivalent to almost four times the speed of a cruise liner.

b During the fall, he travelled at an average speed of 1357.64 kilometres per minute.

c He failed to break the current freefall record.

d Attention was worldwide, with millions watching it on TV.

e It was the first time his parents had travelled outside America.

f He set two other world records.

Felix Baumgartner broke the world's freefall record by jumping 39 kilometres above the earth and breaking the sound barrier.

Felix Baumgartner, a 43-year-old Austrian former military parachutist, floated for two hours in a purpose-built capsule towed by an enormous helium balloon before leaping into the record books from a height equivalent to almost four times the height of a cruising passenger airliner. During the fall, he travelled at an average speed of 1357.64 kilometres per hour.

He broke the current freefall record of 31.3 kilometres held by Joe Kittinger. Mr Kittinger, who set his record in 1960, was the only person allowed to communicate with Mr Baumgartner while he was inside the capsule which carried him into space.

As the launch began, Mr Kittinger told Mr Baumgartner: 'You're doing great, Felix. Doing great. Everything looks green and you are on your way to space.'

Mr Baumgartner's parents were in Roswell, New Mexico for the launch, the first time they had travelled outside of Europe. His mother could be seen weeping as her daredevil son launched into space.

While the action took place in the city of Roswell, famed for space-related incidents, attention was worldwide, with millions watching it online.

Coincidentally, Baumgartner's attempted feat also marked the 65th anniversary of US test pilot Chuck Yeager's successful attempt to become the first man to officially break the sound barrier aboard an aeroplane.

As well as becoming the first man to break the sound barrier unaided, Baumgartner set three other world records during the attempt.

The first came after two hours and two minutes when he broke the record for the highest manned balloon flight, breaking the record of Malcolm Ross and Victor Prather, who soared to 34,668 metres in 1961. Their record ended in tragedy when Prather drowned in the Gulf of Mexico upon landing.

***Adapted from*: www.telegraph.co.uk/science**

5 Read the text again and answer these questions.

a What was Felix's job before he completed this feat?

....

b What two references does the word *leaping* have in the text?

....

c What comparison is given about the height he jumped from?

....

d Who was he in contact with and why was that person also famous?

....

e What had also happened on this day 65 years ago?

....

f What was the first achievement of Felix's feat?

....

g How had the previous record balloon flight ended?

....

h In what way was the colour green significant?

....

D Writing

1 You have decided to tell your school youth club about Felix Baumgartner. First, you need to make some notes in order to prepare your talk. Which **three** of the following headings do you think would be suitable to help you make your notes? Why?

- Home and education
- Nationality
- Physical skills
- Family
- Character
- Achievements

Make **three** notes under each heading.

Example: Home and education

- *Born in Salzburg, Austria.*

Use your notes to write an article for your school newspaper about Felix Baumgartner.

Your article should be 100–150 (Core) or 150–200 (Extended) words long. You will receive up to 6 (Core) / 8 (Extended) marks for the content of your article, and up to 6 (Core) / 8 (Extended) marks for the style and accuracy of your language.

....

....

....

....

....

....

....

....

....

....

....

Unit 14
Medical care

A Vocabulary

1 Complete the crossword.

Across

2 Event that can lead to being hurt (8)

5 Given to aid recovery (10)

7 Vehicle that carries ill people (9)

9 Damage done to the body (6)

10 The care given when someone is ill (9)

Down

1 Trained person who works with the ill (9)

3 The person who receives care when ill (7)

4 The place you stay when ill (8)

6 An urgent situation (9)

8 A person who is injured (8)

2 Match the words with the definitions. Write your answers in the grid

a	b	c	d	e	f	g	h	i	j	k	l	m	n	o
4														

a ~~instability~~	**1** shortage of water
b insecure	**2** people who walk
c ethnic	**3** of more importance than others
d foundation	**4** ~~uncertainty~~
e hygiene	**5** relating to education
f priority	**6** to be carried by this liquid
g waterborne	**7** group with common traditions
h veterinary	**8** stopping or not allowing
i academic	**9** behaving in a sensible way like an adult
j economic	**10** not confident about oneself
k banning	**11** ways to maintain health
l pedestrians	**12** related to animals
m mature	**13** place where someone is going
n destination	**14** the base or the beginning
o drought	**15** related to trade, industry and money

3 Complete the following sentences with words from above.

a Many diseases are ...., which is why they can be spread easily.

b .... have been provided with wide pavements throughout the town.

c She has become very .... about taking her exams and has panic attacks.

d Some people are better suited to .... studies, whereas others prefer something more practical.

e To many people, education is a .... in their lives, and they need to make many sacrifices.

f Many .... students now go to university because they enjoy studying.

g The .... for the new Town Hall were laid over the weekend.

h In many countries, ... people from smoking in public places is very common.

i There are new .... regulations which have to be observed by all restaurant owners.

j The .... resulted in many livestock dying.

4 Use the correct form of either *wound* or *injury* in the following sentences.

- **a** The .... to his body after the car accident resulted in his staying at the hospital for weeks.
- **b** The .... on her hand does not seem to be getting better, so she's going to see a doctor.
- **c** The cat had a .... on its paw and had to be taken to the vet.
- **d** Many people were .... after the earthquake and needed help.
- **e** The .... on his arm was very deep and needed stitches.
- **f** Her .... were severe and could not be dealt with by the paramedic.

B Language focus: future in the past, *practice/practise, advice/advise*

1 Look at this definition of: 'future in the past'. Six words have been put in the wrong place. Underline the wrong words and write the correct one above it.

The use of *will* as the past tense of *would* is often referred to as 'future in the past'. It is used to express the idea that in the future you thought that something else would happen in the past. It does not matter if you are correct or not. Both *was/were going to* and the past continuous can be used to express the past in the future.

2 Underline the 'future in the past' phrases in the examples below. Then number the phrase that (1) describes past events and (2) moves forward in time.

Example: ... (1) <u>the expectation was</u> that (2) she <u>would marry</u> and start a family ...

- **a** When the doctors heard that Florence Nightingale was going to work with them, they felt threatened.
- **b** The doctors felt threatened when they knew she was soon coming to work with them.

3 Circle the best option to complete each sentence.

- **a** The teacher turned up late just as the students **were about to / would** leave.
- **b** You're home late. I thought we **would go / were going** out for dinner.
- **c** I told Pietro that when he arrived at my place, we **would drive / were driving** to the shopping mall.
- **d** Ahmed decided he **would go / will go** to his uncle's house.
- **e** He applied for a different job because he **had planned / was planning** to leave.
- **f** I promised I would **send / to send** this letter yesterday, but I forgot.
- **g** I knew you **would not ask / were not asking** about the homework.
- **h** The teacher was absolutely sure her students **would pass / were passing** their exams.

4 In Unit 14 of the Coursebook you learnt about *practice* and *practise*. Remember that in British English, *practice* is a noun and *practise* is a verb. Complete the sentences using the correct form of either *practice* or *practise*.

- **a** You need to .... playing the piano more if you want to be successful.
- **b** He has a successful .... as a doctor in a small town.
- **c** He wants to .... in a major city first, though, before he goes there.
- **d** Do some more English grammar .... exercises to help you improve.
- **e** The exam .... tests can be found in books which you buy.
- **f** Let him .... speaking without correcting him – it's better.

5 *Advice* and *advise* work in the same way. Complete the following sentences using the correct form of either *advice* or *advise*.

- **a** I think you should .... him about not spending so much money on a car.
- **b** If he had listened to my ...., he would not be having so many problems now.
- **c** I thought the .... they gave was very sensible and I'm going to follow it.
- **d** I .... you not to go to that place as it's dangerous.
- **e** I'd .... you to leave early as the buses are not very regular.
- **f** .... is something you can choose to ignore if you wish.

C Skills

Reading

1 The information in the following sentences comes from one of four texts in Unit 14:

- **i** A career as a paramedic
- **ii** Florence Nightingale
- **iii** ICRC
- **iv** Traffic

Write the title of the text next to each sentence.

Example: Medical facilities for wounded soldiers were criticised. Florence Nightingale

- **a** Other forms of transport can be used to get to patients. ....
- **b** The impact upon less developed countries is much greater. ....
- **c** Many millions have and continue to die due to this development. ....
- **d** They are normally the first professionals to arrive on the scene. ....

e She did a three-month training course in Germany. ....

f They normally work in pairs. ....

g They are strongly motivated by the nature of their humanitarian work. ....

h They provide an immediate response. ....

i An inspiring person who influenced modern health care. ....

j Preference is given to provision of essential goods before health care. ....

k Born in Italy in 1820. ....

l It provides more than just help in a crisis. ....

m The crisis has reached catastrophic proportions. ....

n They adapt their response to suit the context. ....

o The damage to their health and economic potential will affect them for life. ....

D Listening

1 You are going to listen to two people talking about their different experiences in nursing. Before you listen, look at the words and phrases in the box. Check the meaning of any words you are unsure about.

community nurse	cultural	specialised in	experience
rewarding	orthopaedic	mental health	

2 Which words and phrases from Exercise D1 do you think best complete the notes below about what the two people say?

Modern matron **(a)** .... dealing with **(b)** .... issues and how they can be influenced by **(c)** .... and ethnic factors.

Very **(d)** .... dealing with and helping people to get their lives back together again.

Relief **(e)** .... has progressed from working in hospitals with cancer and **(f)** .... patients to visiting people in their homes, clinics and nursing homes.

Good idea to get **(g)** .... before getting into nursing.

3 **CD2, Track 21** You will hear two people talking about their nursing careers. Listen to what they say and look at the questions. For each question choose the correct answer, A, B or C, and put a tick in the appropriate box. You will hear the talk twice.

1 He became a matron because:

A he loved working with elderly people. ☐

B he hated banking. ☐

C a family member was very keen. ☐

2 He chose to specialise in mental health because:

- **A** he loved to be involved with his patients. ☐
- **B** the patients don't wear uniforms. ☐
- **C** he did a diploma in that area. ☐

3 He became qualified to work in his present job by:

- **A** going to university and spending some time doing the course. ☐
- **B** understanding how people's backgrounds influence them. ☐
- **C** working in a private hospital. ☐

4 People with mental health issues:

- **A** don't like going to work on Mondays. ☐
- **B** have problems finding their way in life. ☐
- **C** use their skills to get better. ☐

5 The relief community nurse:

- **A** was frustrated only looking after her child. ☐
- **B** thought her children would be her lifelong career. ☐
- **C** wanted nursing as a career. ☐

6 In her first year as a qualified nurse:

- **A** she worked with patients who were very ill. ☐
- **B** she was on her feet a lot. ☐
- **C** she was rewarded for being organised. ☐

7 From dealing with patients with cancer:

- **A** she worked in a hospital orthopaedic ward. ☐
- **B** she visited places outside a hospital. ☐
- **C** she only dealt with eight patients. ☐

8 By working in people's environments:

- **A** she makes them realistic about their illness. ☐
- **B** she can test and educate patients. ☐
- **C** she is aware of related appropriate conditions. ☐

Unit 15
Healthy living

A Vocabulary

1 Fill in the missing letters to create phrases from Unit 15 of your Coursebook.

a a _ l _ _ _ _ r of flowers

b nervous _ y _ _ _ m

c E _ _ _ t _ _ _ hieroglyphs

d couch _ _ t _ _ o _ _

e r _ _ u _ _ _ stress

f no pain no _ _ _ n

g aesthetic a _ _ _ _ l

h high blood _ r _ s _ _ _ _

i honey and _ _ n _ _ _

j dietary _ u p _ _ _ _ _ _ _ _

k intense _ r _ m _ _ _ _ flavours

l perennial _ l _ _ _

m mineral c _ _ _ _ _ t

n nature's _ h _ _ m _ _ _

o seventeenth _ e _ _ _ _ _

2 Use the correct form of phrases in Exercise A1 to complete the following sentences.

a .... are normally those that last for a very long time.

b Many feel that if you eat a balanced diet, then you shouldn't need to take ....

c At the gym I go to they believe that you need to push yourself to get results and they say ....

d .... were a pictorial form of communication developed around 3300 BCE.

e Teenagers are sometimes called .... because they just sit watching TV.

f Yoga and doing exercise are often seen as effective ways of ....

g Every year .... would grow round the base of the tree in our garden.

h Eating ginger and garlic are seen as part of .... because of their health benefits.

i Edible flowers can sometimes be put on food not only because of their .... but also because of the nutrients they contain.

j Middle Eastern cooking is popular and famous for its ....

3 In the following sentences, four of the words in **bold** have been used incorrectly. Tick [✓] the sentences that are correct and correct the mistakes.

a **Bicycling** means the same as cycling. ....

b The **structure** of a sentence is how it is formed. ....

c If you walk **strenuously** then you are using a lot of energy. ....

d **Joints** are parts of the body that don't move and are fixed. ....

e The **abdomen** is another word for stomach. ....

f **Intonation** in speech is influenced by your nationality. ....

g **Hoeing** is where you water plants with a hose pipe. ....

h **China** is both a country and a material used to make plates, cups, etc. ....

....

i **Therapeutic** treatment would aim to relax you. ....

j The **branches** on a tree are where the leaves don't grow. ....

4 Complete the following sentences with either *intensity* or *strength*.

a He played the violin with great ...., producing a most beautiful piece of work.

b She sat and stared at him with such .... that he felt quite uncomfortable and lowered his eyes.

c .... has to be important when you're doing manual work as otherwise it'll be too difficult.

d Many are against the idea of women joining the army as they feel they don't have enough ....

e The course was too short and needed to be run with such .... that many of the trainees had to give up.

f Lions are incredible animals and hunt and run with such .... that they are real kings of the jungle.

B Language focus: quantifiers, fillers

1 Use one of the following quantifiers to complete each of the following sentences.

a lot of	a couple of	the majority of	a mix of	a little	a number of
a variety of	a minority of	a pair of	a great deal	plenty of	several

a There are .... cakes to choose from but you're only allowed one.

b Would you add .... more sugar to my tea please?

c .... people have asked that we finish early.

d Only .... the population have voted in the referendum.

e There is .... sweet and savoury desserts to suit all tastes.

f He's having .... of trouble passing his driving test.

g .... the records are out of date and so we're throwing them away.

h Although the garden is very bare, there are .... nice trees in it.

i .... people have donated to the charity and it is doing quite well now.

j He tried on .... black trousers but they did not go with the jacket.

k She looked after the garden well, although .... plants have died.

l We voted on the school trip and .... students chose the seaside.

2 Using the following quantifying phrases from Exercise B1, write five of your own sentences.

a The majority of ....

b A minority of ....

c A lot of ....

d A variety of ....

e A number of ....

3 **CD2, Track 22** Listen again to Track 7 from Activity E4 in Unit 15 and answer the following questions about the fillers and introductory phrases they use.

Speaker 1

a What does she mean when she says *To be honest* . . .?

....

b By saying *I don't think* . . . what does she actually think about her lifestyle nowadays?

....

c What reason does she give for the state of her lifestyle and what filler does she use to predict the reason?

....

d How does she contradict what she said earlier with . . . *having said that* . . .?

....

Speaker 2

a How do we know that her friends are busy people?

....

b Which filler or phrase is used to stress this idea of 'busy'?

....

Speaker 3

a By using *obviously* what kind of statement is being made?

....

b By using *But in my opinion* ... is the speaker agreeing or not with 'a'?

....

c By saying *So it's probably not a bad idea* ... is she accepting or rejecting the ideas?

....

Speaker 4

a Does *It seems to me* ... express an opinion or a feeling?

....

b Who is she asking *Is it worth it*?

....

Speaker 5

a What different fillers and phrases does he use to express his opinion about the topic?

....

b What filler or phrase does he use to express his feeling of uselessness at the situation?

....

C Skills

Reading

1 You are now going to read a text about asthma and what triggers it. Use a reference to complete the two sentences below:

a Asthma is ....

b *Triggers* means ....

2 Now read the text and underline all the examples of the two words that you can find. How many examples are there of:

a Asthma ....

b Triggers ....

Dealing with asthma triggers

What's a trigger?

People with asthma have what's called a chronic or continuing problem with their airways (the breathing tubes in their lungs), which are swollen and full of mucus. This problem is made worse by asthma triggers, such as animal hair, exercise or smoke.

Triggers are substances, weather conditions or activities that are harmless to most people. But in people with asthma, they can lead to coughing, wheezing and shortness of breath. Triggers don't actually cause asthma (no one knows exactly what does cause it), but triggers can lead to asthma symptoms and flare-ups.

Every person with asthma has different triggers. That's why cats may cause one person's asthma to flare up, but have no impact at all on someone else. Some people have one or two triggers; others have a dozen. Triggers are sometimes seasonal and may even stop affecting a teen with asthma as he or she gets older.

Common asthma triggers include:

- colds or the flu
- allergens (things that cause allergic reactions, such as animal hair and plant pollen)
- irritants in the air (such as perfume, smoke and air pollution)
- weather conditions
- exercise.

Coping with common triggers

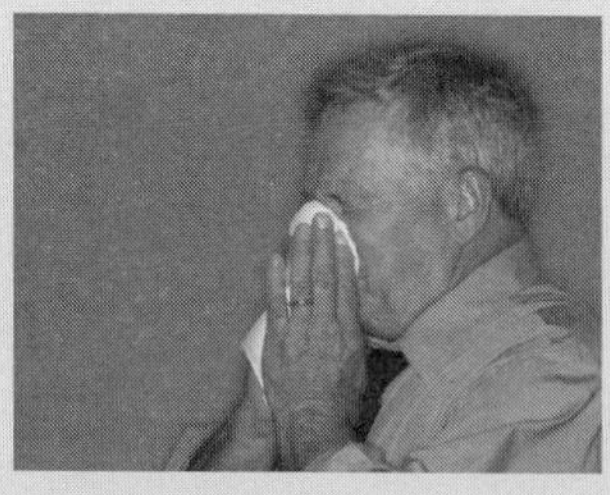

Allergens are one of the most common asthma triggers. Allergens include mould, dust mites, cockroaches and pollen, and from animals: skin flakes, saliva, urine and feathers. If you think you might have an allergy, talk to a parent or doctor about getting allergy testing.

In addition to other treatments for allergies, doctors recommend avoiding allergens. It isn't possible to avoid everything, of course, but there are some things you can do:

- Keep your room as clean and dust free as possible – this means vacuuming and dusting weekly and getting rid of clutter. Your old stuffed animals and prize ribbons may need to go into a box in the attic.
- Wash your sheets weekly in hot water and get rid of feather pillows and comforters. You can get covers for your mattress and pillows that will help too.
- Get rid of carpets and curtains. Rugs, carpeting and other heavy fabrics can trap allergens that make you ill.

If you have allergies that worsen your asthma, you might also need to take medication or have allergy injections. Your doctor will let you know. In some extreme cases, it may be necessary to receive treatment in a hospital or clinic, but the number of people who need this has dropped considerably over the past 20 years or so, as these statistics about hospital visits for people in Australia show.

Irritants are different from allergens because they can also affect people who don't have allergies or asthma. For most people, irritants don't create a serious problem, but for people with asthma, they can lead to flare-ups. Common irritants include perfumes, aerosol sprays, cleaning products, wood and tobacco smoke, paint or gas fumes and air pollution. Even things that may seem harmless, such as scented candles or glue, are triggers for some people.

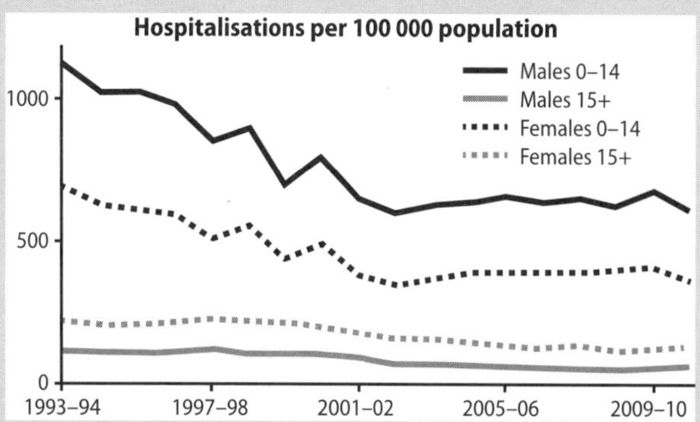

Hospital visits for asthma sufferers per 100 000 of the population

If you notice that a household product triggers your asthma, ask your family to switch to an unscented or non-aerosol version of it. If smoke bothers you, obviously people smoking around you will be a trigger. But a fire in the fireplace or woodstove can also be a problem.

If outdoor air pollution is a trigger for your asthma, running the air conditioner can help. You can check air-quality reports on the news to monitor which days might be bad for you. Then, on days when the quality is especially bad, you can stay in air-conditioned comfort, whether it's at your house or the mall.

Adapted from*: *http://kidshealth.org

3 Now look at the questions below and write the answers.

a What and where are the 'airways'? [1]

....

b What actually causes asthma? [1]

....

c Why might a cat trigger asthma in one person but not in another? [1]

....

d How many asthma triggers do people have? [1]

....

e What advice is given for people who think they might have an allergy? [1]

....

f If an asthma attack is particularly serious, what might be necessary? [1]

....

g According to the diagram, which age groups are most likely to receive hospital treatment? [1]

....

h How are irritants different from allergens? Give an example of each. [1]

....

i What should someone do if a household product triggers asthma symptoms? [1]

....

Extended

j According to doctors, what can be done to avoid allergens? Give **four** pieces of advice. [4]

....

....

....

....

....

....

[Total: 13 Extended, 9 Core]

D Listening

1 **CD2, Track 23** Look again at the speaking topic card for Unit 15 in your Coursebook and listen to two students discussing how they would respond to the prompts. As you listen, decide whether George or Caroline expresses each opinion (a–g). In some cases, you may need to choose **both** George **and** Caroline. You will hear the conversation twice.

> **Lifestyle changes**
>
> There have been many changes in the way people live in the past one hundred years.
>
> Discuss this topic.
>
> *Use the following prompts, in the order given below, to develop the conversation:*
>
> - things that you have today that people one hundred years ago had no idea about
> - your idea of a healthy lifestyle compared to your grandparents' lifestyles
> - standards of living and differences in income and possessions
> - opportunities to know more about healthy living and different lifestyles
> - the idea that people in the past had a much better understanding of a healthy lifestyle than we do today.
>
> You may introduce related ideas of your own to expand on these prompts.
>
> Remember, you are not allowed to make any written notes.

Which person, George or Caroline …

a won't have a problem talking about the topic card? ....

b thinks that technology has had a big impact on modern life? ....

c is very surprised at how older people use social media? ....

d says that older people in their families have had a healthy lifestyle? ....

e cannot understand why people buy so many things? ....

f gets information at school about healthy living? ....

g thinks that people do not pay attention to advice about healthy living? ....

Unit 16

Social media

A Vocabulary

1 Below is a list of things that you can do with a mobile phone. Put the letters in the correct order to find out what they are.

a send or c e e v r i e .... text messages

b t c k k a e r p e .... of appointments

c a p y l .... games

d n s d e .... emails

e o e s t r .... contact information

f o w l d d a n o .... information from the internet

g h a c w t .... TV

h s e u .... the built-in calculator

i e t a k .... pictures

j t g e .... apps

k e a k m .... videos

l v s e a .... reminders

2 Write three more things, not on the list, that you can use your phone for.

a ....

b ....

c ....

3 In Unit 16 you saw and learnt these words. Find out what they are according to the code (1–26).

1	2	3	4	5	6	7	8	9	10	11	12	13	14	15
a	b	c	d	e	f	g	h	i	j	k	l	m	n	o

16	17	18	19	20	21	22	23	24	25	26
p	q	r	s	t	u	v	w	x	y	z

Example: 4 9 19 3 <u>d i s c</u>

a 1 2 19 20 1 9 14 5 4 _ _ _ _ _ _ _ _ _

b 3 15 13 16 21 12 19 9 22 5 12 25 _ _ _ _ _ _ _ _ _ _ _ _

c 1 22 9 4 – 13 21 12 20 9 20 1 19 11 5 18 19 _ _ _ _ – _ _ _ _ _ _ _ _ _ _ _ _ _

d 13 9 14 4 – 2 15 7 7 12 9 14 7 _ _ _ _ – _ _ _ _ _ _ _ _

e 19 5 12 6 – 5 19 20 5 5 13 _ _ _ _ – _ _ _ _ _ _

f 19 21 16 16 18 5 19 19 5 4 _ _ _ _ _ _ _ _ _ _

g 20 18 1 9 20 19 _ _ _ _ _ _

h 19 5 4 5 14 20 1 18 25 _ _ _ _ _ _ _ _ _ _

i 4 5 20 18 9 13 5 14 20 1 12 _ _ _ _ _ _ _ _ _ _ _ _ _

j 16 18 15 6 15 21 14 4 _ _ _ _ _ _ _ _ _

k 7 1 21 7 5 _ _ _ _ _

l 16 18 5 3 21 18 19 15 18 19 _ _ _ _ _ _ _ _ _ _ _ _

4 Now select words from Exercise A3 to complete these sentences.

a They are called couch potatoes because they lead such a .... life.

b He .... from voting as he couldn't decide which party to choose.

c You should be able to .... whether it's ready just by looking at it.

d There was a .... choice of cat food in the supermarket.

e They play those video games .... and I don't think it's healthy.

f It's .... to your health when you only eat fast food as it contains a lot of salt.

g There are always .... of how well a person will perform in tests if you continuously assess them.

h Some people can only focus on one task at a time whereas others thrive on being ....

5 Choose either *according to*, *depending on* or *while* to complete the sentences.

a He plans to go to the museum, ... whether he can get away from work early.

b .... the weather forecast today, there might be showers this afternoon.

c They were eating their dinner .... they were playing that stupid game and so they had no idea about what they were eating!

d The colour of that dress really suits you, ... the shape of the other is much better.

e Well, ... Andreas, you didn't arrive until after the film had started!

f .... your availability, we'll meet at some point next week.

g She wants to go to university, ... her examination grades.

h They were swimming in the sea .... it was raining and thought that it was wonderful.

i .... whether or not we finish this work, we'll decide about the cinema later.

B Language focus: *-ing* forms

1 Which **eight** words from the ten in the list can be spelled using the letters in the box? You can use each letter more than once. Write down each word.

falling chatting texting taking using shocking lying spending stopping ~~going~~	n d t c s k e i h u x g a p o

Example: G O I N G

a ....

b ....

c ....

d ....

e ....

f ....

g ....

2 Look again at the ten words in Exercise B1. Underline the **five** words whose base spelling changes when *-ing* is added. Write the five words below in both forms.

Example: amaze – amazing

a ....

b ....

c ....

d ....

e ....

3 Look at the sentences below and match each one with its form.

a As a verb after a preposition	**i** Sewing, knitting, reading – they're all her hobbies.
b As sentence subject	**ii** They like watching films at home together.
c To list activities	**iii** After having a shower, I went to bed.
d To add information in a clause	**iv** They are waiting for the bus in the rain.
e In continuous tenses	**v** Cooking is one of her favourite hobbies.
f After certain verbs	**vi** She wandered off, speaking on her phone.

4 Write six sentences using *-ing* in each of the six different forms from Exercise B3.

....

....

....

....

....

....

C Skills

Reading

1 You are going to read an internet article about social networks for teenagers. Before you read the article look at the questions a–j and choose one of the following forms of social media. Each one may be chosen more than once.

A Twitter

B Facebook

C Snapchat

D Instagram

a It is currently the most successful. ....

b It does not appeal as much to young people. ....

c About twelve months ago it was most favoured by young people. ....

d Presently it is almost equal in popularity. ....

e Increased use by older people has made it less trendy. ....

f An alternative and more recent social media. ....

g It still hasn't reached the level of its main competitor. ....

h It is connected to one of the main forms of social media. ....

i This suits a specific market and is becoming popular. ....

j It had never been the owner's intention for it to be hip. ....

2 Now decide if these four statements are true or false. Give reasons.

a Teens rated Twitter the 'most important' social media network, with Facebook and Instagram close behind. True / False

....

b Last year, Facebook was rated the most important by 42% of teens. True / False

....

c This year, Facebook was rated the most important site by only 23% of teens. True / False

....

d Teens told researchers they dislike Facebook because of 'drama', too many adult users and other users 'over-sharing'. True / False

....

3 Quickly skim the internet article below and see if your answers for Exercises C1 and C2 were correct.

Twitter overtakes Facebook as the most popular social network for teens, according to study

[1] Mark Zuckerberg admitted it and a new study has proved it: Facebook is no longer cool with teens. The semi-annual 'Taking Stock with Teens' study indicated that Twitter has overtaken Facebook as the most important social media network. Last year, 42% of teens rated Facebook as the most important social media network, while this year only 23% rated it as the most influential. Twitter was rated by 26% of teens as their 'most important' social media site. Not to be outdone, the Facebook-owned Instagram also garnered 23% of votes, up from 12% last year.

[2] The study, by investment firm Piper Jaffray, gathers information relating to teen spending patterns, fashion trends, and brand and media preferences. Another study, Pew's Teens, Social Media and Privacy report, had similar findings. Pew's focus groups said the popularity of Facebook is waning because of parental and adult use of the site, other users 'over-sharing' and 'drama' that can erupt between Facebook 'friends'. According to Pew's research, despite its lack of 'cool', teens continue to use Facebook because 'participation is an important part of overall teenage socialising'. The study also noted that teens have an average of 300 Facebook friends, but only 79 Twitter followers.

[3] 'I got mine [Facebook account] around sixth grade. And I was really obsessed with it for a while. Then towards eighth grade, things changed. Once you get into Twitter, if you make Twitter and Instagram accounts, then you'll just kind of forget about Facebook. That's what I did,' one teen told Pew researchers.

[4] Zuckerberg himself may concur with teens who think Facebook is no longer cool.

'People assume that we're trying to be cool. It's never been my goal. I'm the least cool person there is! We're almost ten years old, so we're definitely not a niche thing any more, so that kind of angle for coolness is done for us,' he said in September. Instead of being cool, he wants Facebook to be a tool people use every day, 'like electricity'.

[5] 17% responded in the category marked 'other', and this indicates that other niche social media sites, such as Snapchat and Vine, are taking off in a big way with teens.

***Adapted from*: www.dailymail.co.uk**

4 Find words or phrases in the article that have a similar meaning to the following.

a important or significant (paragraph 1) ....

b not wanting to be beaten (1) ....

c won or gained (1) ....

d fanatical or passionate (3) ....

e agree (4) ....

f special product (4) ....

5 What do the following numbers in paragraph 1 refer to?

Example: 42 is the percentage of teens who rated Facebook as the most important social media last year.

a 23 ....

b 26 ....

c 23 (again) ....

d 12 ....

Unit 17

The environment

A Vocabulary

1 Complete the definitions with the words and phrases from the box.

bloc	fertiliser	have a glimpse	discarded	future prosperity
consensus	curtailed	ecology	beverage	exotic
biodegradable	vulnerable			

a .... is a word which describes different types of hot and cold drinks.

b .... means something can be broken down naturally to avoid pollution.

c .... also means to throw away or to get rid of.

d A parrot, certain fruits like star fruit, papaya and mangoes are all seen as being ....

e .... is the science that looks at organisms and their environment.

f A group of countries or political parties with common interests can be referred to as a ....

g A .... is where all involved have to agree before a decision can be made.

h When you .... of something, you only see it briefly.

i When you are .... from doing something, then you are restricted.

j A .... person is one who is easily hurt and weak both physically and emotionally.

k The .... of a country can be affected by many events in the world.

l .... is used in soil and plants so that they grow more quickly and larger.

2 Choose words from Exercise A1 to complete the following sentences.

a Many .... have been banned from being used on crops as they can be dangerous to humans.

b They love fish and have some .... ones from Asia in their aquarium.

c The kittens were very .... as they had been left alone by their mother for days.

d The idea of introducing a new school uniform was .... because of the cost to parents.

e You can .... of my wedding dress but not the whole thing, as I want it to be a surprise.

f The freedom of the students out of school hours had been .... due to some bad behaviour.

g They reached a .... on how to divide the money equally between the different charities.

h Plastic bags are not very .... and are a huge problem for marine life where they're thrown in the sea.

3 Complete the sentences using the correct form of either *affect* or *effect*.

a The teacher said that this test would have no .... on our final grade.

b I did not expect the film to .... me in the negative way it did.

c I did not let his anger .... me like it had last time.

d The.. of the light in the room is very pleasing.

e His absences from school are starting to .... his grades.

f The new school regulations had the desired ....

g Loud music in a film gives the .... that something is about to happen.

h How much a student studies definitely .... his grades in a positive way.

B Language focus: introductory phrases, referring words

1 Complete the sentences using the following phrases. Use a different one for each sentence.

- (It) looks/seems like …
- (It) looks/seems as if/though …
- (It) looks like …
- (It) looks/seems …

a .... the President is coming to the theatre tonight.

b The portrait .... so beautiful but in reality it's hiding a secret.

c .... the computer needs fixing again.

d .... they are coming early from what Mary said.

e That dress .... wrong on her because of the colours.

f .... not enough votes were cast for them to win.

g .... a beautiful day is expected today.

h .... we won't be going after all as they forgot to buy tickets.

i The sky's gone grey; .... rain is on the way.

2 Now write your own sentences using each of the forms twice.

3 In Unit 17, you looked at *referring words*. You were given boxed words and asked which word or words they were referring back to. Now look back at the passage 'A dangerous thirst' in Unit 17 Exam focus and write what each of the following words is referring to:

a Line 5–6 'a condition' ....

b Line 14 'he' ....

c Line 18 'Those' ....

d Line 19 'they' ....

e Line 24 'those' ....

f Line 39 'they' ....

g Line 40 'there' ....

h Line 44 'her' ....

i Line 50 'them' ....

C Skills

Reading

1 You are going to read a report written by young people. In this report, people were asked: *What does climate change mean to young people?* Before you read the report, write notes for each of the questions (a–d).

a What is climate change?

....

....

b How do you think climate change impacts your life?

....

....

c In what ways are you aware of changes to the climate (this could be in your country or abroad)?

....

....

d Which countries in the world, do you think, have been the worst affected by climate change?

....

....

2 The report claims: *'Climate change is a global problem and is set to hit the youngest hardest, particularly in developing states.'* Decide if the following statements about climate change are true or false.

a Climate change has affected most countries. True / False

b Governments always support young people's efforts to help the environment. True / False

c Developing countries are the worst affected because they have fewer resources. True / False

d There is little effort and change being made by many countries to improve the situation. True / False

3 Skim the text below and decide which country (India, France, Peru, Rwanda) is being talked about in each section (a–d). Give two reasons for each of your choices.

India	~~France~~	Peru	Rwanda

a *France*

  i *Because he uses the French words: modèle social.*

  ii ....

b ....

  i ....

  ii ....

c ....

  i ....

  ii ....

d ....

  i ....

  ii ....

[a] Antoine Ebel, 22, ...

The report doesn't change much. It confirms what we already knew – human activities have a catastrophic influence on our climate. Whether we are 90% or 95% certain of that is mostly irrelevant.

Our duty as young people is to highlight the solutions, imagining, describing and starting to build a climate-friendly world that people will want to live in – demonstrating that climate change is also a chance to start things fresh, rethink and rebuild our societies on more solid and sustainable bases.

I also think that we need to realise, as a country, that climate change is affecting us too and that was obvious this year with the flooding of the Seine. It's not just about us being 'charitable' to small islands and polar bears when we reduce our emissions; we're also keeping our modèle social alive.

[b] Alexandra Gavilano, 24, ...

In ...., climate change is noticeable by various changes in the local weather. In the highlands of the Andean mountains, heavy rains called *huaico* by the local people, with never-seen-before tennis-ball-sized hailstones, destroy the houses and infrastructure of the small towns.

But the rain doesn't stay in the mountains. In February, the city of Trujillo was partially flooded, shutting down the electricity and infrastructure in parts of the city. Parts of the Chan Chan sandstone ruins were destroyed. Rain now falls in an area that was distinct for centuries for its dry and hot weather.

It's interesting that a lot of youngsters in ...., either in universities or doing art on the street, want to make a change, but feel stopped by the national government, which has shown heavy threats with military forces against people standing up against governmental interests.

[c] Neeshad V. S., 26, ...

The implications of the report are of utmost importance to .... as well as the rest of the world.

Climate change impacts can be seen on various sectors across Asia, including ....

The frequency of more intense rainfall events in many parts of Asia has increased, causing severe floods, landslides, debris and mud flows, while the numbers of rainy days have decreased. This is shown in the Western Ghats which are a range of mountains which have a big impact on the tropical climate of the region and where the level of rainfall has risen dramatically in past years.

With over 400 LEED-certified buildings and many states adopting the Energy Conservation Building Code (ECBC), ... continues to make strides in reducing its carbon emissions. .... can also create a low-carbon development path by shifting to clean energy. Progress made to achieve ....'s National Solar Mission is one example of the way forward, though much more needs to be done to continue ....'s rapid growth sustainably.

This undeniable evidence of human-caused warming and the catastrophic results of inaction should spur the world's largest and oldest democracies into seizing this urgent opportunity for cooperation.

[d] Yves Tuyishime, 27, ...

Africa is one of the most vulnerable continents to climate change and has lower adaptive capacity. Most African economies depend on agriculture and changing weather threatens African agriculture.

It is obvious that Africa is not only being affected by emissions 'made in Africa'. Presently, Africa's contribution towards global emissions is relatively small compared to emissions from the developed world. Nonetheless, as we know based on our awareness of increasing levels of air pollution as in the capital Kigali, we cannot become complacent and blame others for what is obviously becoming more of a home-made problem as well.

But no matter how much mitigation effort Africa puts in, it remains insignificant unless industrialised countries do something. Therefore, we are calling for action by developed countries so that we can then follow suit.

***Adapted from*: www.rtcc.org**

4 Look back at the statements (a–d) in Exercise C2. Scan the text to find out whether you made the correct decisions.

5 Answer these questions about the text.

a Why does Antoine give the two figures? What is he trying to stress?

....

b What is Antoine referring to with the expression modèle social?

....

c What does Alexandra say about the area that was once distinct?

....

d Why are heavy threats and military force used against the young people in Peru?

....

e What has been reduced in Asia?

....

f Who does Neeshad suggest should encourage other countries to work together?

....

g Why does Yves think Africa improving its environment will not have much world impact?

....

h What unwittingly is being imported into Africa and having an impact on its economy?

....

6 You have been asked by your teacher to make a presentation to students entitled: *What does climate change mean to young people in my country?* You need to make notes in order to prepare. Make your notes under each heading.

Main environmental issues in my country

- ....
- ....
- ....

How the environment has changed in my country

- ....
- ....

What efforts (if any) are being made to improve the environment in my country?

- ....
- ....

Other

- ....
- ....
- ....

D Writing

1 Imagine that you have given your presentation and now your teacher wants you to write a follow-up report, based on your notes. Write three paragraphs, using your notes from the first three headings in C6. Your summary should be about 100 words long. You should use your own words as far as possible.

....

....

....

....

....

....

....

....

....

....

....

....

A Vocabulary

1 Complete the table with the following words. Which word is hidden in the vertical column? The first letter has been given to you.

biotechnology / dynamic / innovative / alleviating / invent / manipulated / confectionery / consumption / discard / dispose

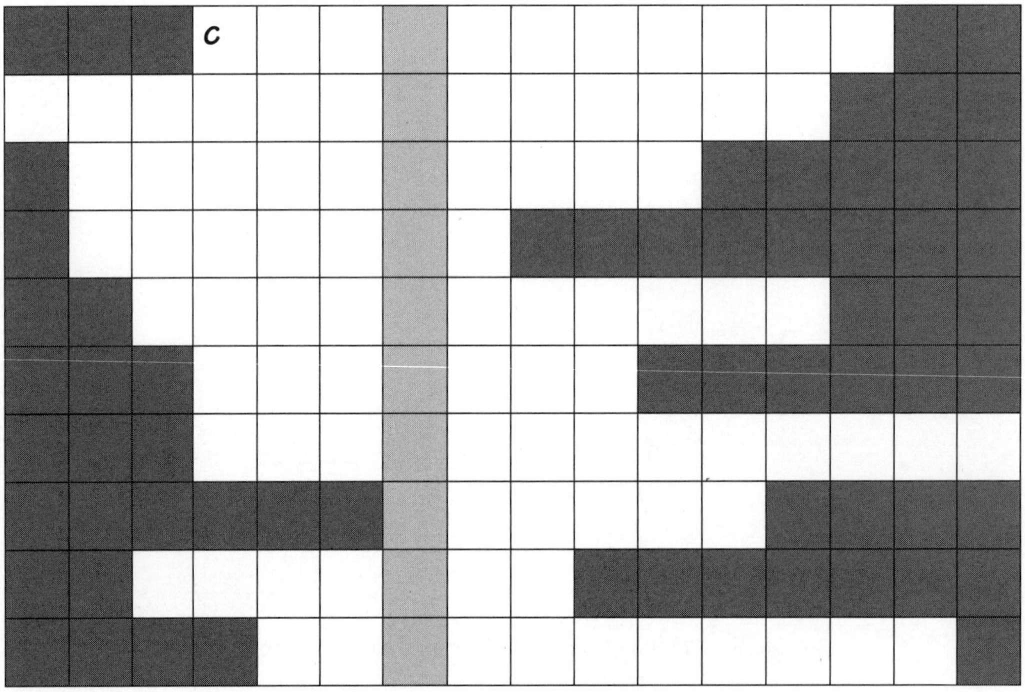

2 Match the words from Exercise A1 with the definitions below.

a Making something less of a problem or less severe. ....

b To throw out or get rid of something. ....

c Took advantage of or controlled skilfully. ....

d To create for the first time. ....

e The action of using up a resource, whether food or electricity. ....

f Sweets and chocolates. ....

g Featuring new methods; advanced and original. ....

h Characterised by constant change, activity or progress. ....

i The use of animal and plant cells for industrial or scientific purposes. ....

j .... of: a synonym for **2b**. ....

3 Find the 18 words in the word circle from Unit 18 and then write each one in the correct category.

concentrationinventivestarvepreparedalleviateinnovativepreparationconcentrateinnovatorinnovateconcentratedstarvationinventalleviationalleviatedstarvinginventorprepare

Noun	Verb	Adjective
	alleviate	

4 Now choose words from the table above to complete the sentences.

a The .... meal from the supermarket had hardly any flavour.

b The .... on his face as he worked hard to get the essay finished, was painful.

c To .... the effect of the headache, you should try lying down in a dark room.

d The levels of .... in the world have been decreasing in past years.

e To .... something technically new nowadays is actually very difficult.

f The idea of using a robot for cleaning was ....

g The .... for the Olympic games can take many years and a lot of money.

h He was .... when he came home from school as he had not eaten since breakfast.

5 Complete the sentences using either *breath* or *breathe*.

a His .... came out short and panicky when he saw the bear.

b The doctor always asks me to .... deeply to hear if my lungs are healthy.

c It's best to .... slowly and deeply when you are frightened about something.

d The wind was like a .... of fresh air in the humid weather.

e His .... became heavier and more laboured as he climbed the mountain.

f On a cold day you can see your .... when you ....

g I find that I can .... better in the countryside where the air is cleaner.

h His .... smelt strongly of garlic after the meal.

B Language focus: sequence markers

1 Match the sequence markers (a–f) with the descriptions (i–vi).

a consequently / so / as a result

b furthermore / in addition / what is more

c first / secondly / thirdly / to begin with / next / after that / finally

d likewise / similarly

e nevertheless / in any case / for all that / all the same

f conversely / on the contrary / by way of contrast

i They can indicate chronological order, or order of importance

ii They can add to or reinforce what has already been said

iii They can indicate that two ideas are equal

iv They can indicate cause–result relationships

v They can indicate that a given idea contradicts another

vi They can indicate compromise

2 Use the correct sequence markers to complete the paragraph.

The municipality is going to plan a children's playground in an urban area but **(a)** .... we're going to plan a rural one as well.

The board agreed to all of the architect's concerns about the playgrounds, but **(b)** .... still think that he's being very demanding.

(c) ...., we've decided that the situation, where we will use his assistance and guidance, can only be temporary and we'll use our own professionals in the future.

And **(d)**.., we've agreed with our colleagues at the municipality that finances will have to be controlled now as the architect is very expensive. **(e)** .... his control of labour and who does what will now have to be checked by us for the same reasons.

So this is what we're going to do: **(f)** .... we'll decide who will manage the project; **(g)** ....

3 Look at the sketches of how to make a loaf of bread, which are in the wrong order. First you need to match the correctly ordered recipe instructions with each sketch.

☐ 

☐ 

☐ 

☐ 

☐ 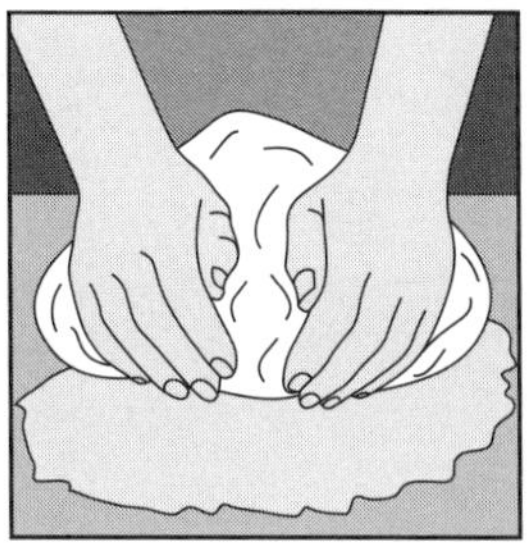

☐ 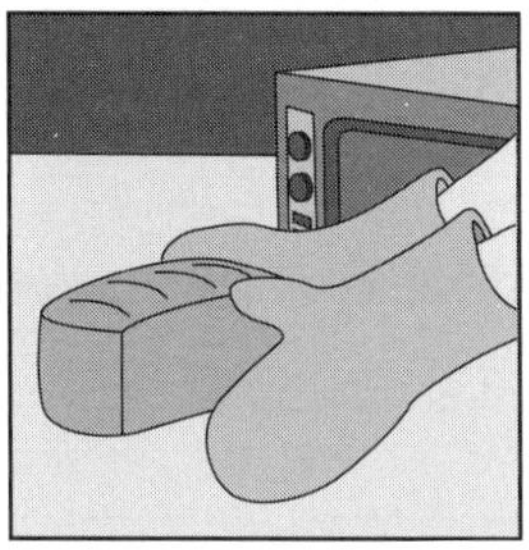

☐ 

a Weigh the ingredients, i.e. flour, yeast, water, etc.

b Mix the ingredients well until they form a dough.

c Leave the dough to sit until it has doubled in size.

d Work the dough again and put onto a baking tray.

e Leave about 40 minutes for a second rise.

f Put the dough into a hot oven and bake for about 40 minutes.

g Remove from the oven and cool.

4 Now imagine that you are describing how to make a loaf of bread to someone. In order to do that clearly you need to use sequence markers. Write your description.

To begin with, you weigh ....

....

....

....

....

....

....

....

....

....

....

C Skills

Reading

1 Reread the text 'Satisfying our hunger is bad for planet Earth' in Unit 18 of the Coursebook and answer the following questions.

  a Apart from production processes, what else about food is bad for planet Earth?

  ....

  b How many food culprits are listed?

  ....

  c Which part of the world is particularly at risk from sugar production?

  ....

  d Give **two** ways in which sugar production pollutes the environment.

  ....

  ....

  e Why is fast-food transportation a problem for the Earth?

  ....

  f Other than people, what else might be affected by groundwater pollution?

  ....

  g How many people rely on rice as part of their daily food?

  ....

  h Identify **one** similarity between sugar and rice production.

  ....

2 You are going to read an article called 'Should cooking be taught at school?' First, answer the following questions.

  a Can you cook? If yes, what can you cook? If no, would you like to learn? Why, or why not?

  ....

  ....

  b Do you think that cookery should be taught at school? Why, or why not?

  ....

  ....

  c If you were to learn to cook at school, what exactly do you think you should learn – for example how to make coffee, the nutritional value of food?

  ....

  ....

  d What other subjects do you think should be taught at your school? List at least two.

  ....

  ....

3 Look at the following points. Decide if they are in favour of cookery classes at school or not in favour. Put a tick or a cross in the box.

- **a** It is one of the basic skills in life and everyone should be taught it. ☐
- **b** It is not necessary to learn because somebody already has these skills at home. ☐
- **c** There are much more important things to learn. ☐
- **d** Food is not made like that nowadays, so what's the point in learning cookery? ☐
- **e** It should be part of learning about a healthy lifestyle. ☐
- **f** I'm just not interested. ☐

4 Look at these phrases from the text. Write the number for the phrase to fill in the gaps in the article.

1. … for the best chef …
2. … a healthy lifestyle as by studying nutrition, …
3. … merely a female domain, as some of …
4. … and unable to take care of themselves.
5. Thus, it is important for students …
6. … could develop in an area not exposed to before.

Should cooking be taught at school? by Chan Chi Man, Cathy

Children nowadays are often blamed for being spoiled **(a)** .... A compulsory home economics course is an effective method to address this problem.

By learning basic skills like cooking, cleaning and money management, students can learn how to take care of themselves. We know that when parents become older or die, children need to live independently and look after their own families. **(b)** .... to come to grips with these important skills early in life. To make sure that all students – regardless of gender and age – learn these skills, a compulsory home economics class is a must.

This can also help them develop **(c)** .... they are more likely to have a balanced diet instead of consuming fast food and ready-made meals, which contain a lot of fat, salt and sugar.

On top of that, children should have more opportunities to develop different interests. Not everybody wants to study Mathematics and Physics, for example. So, students who are not academically or scientifically inclined **(d)** ....
There is increasingly a general acceptance that 'food' and 'cookery' have now become buzz words and there is a lot of excitement about the industry and the opportunities there. Catering or cookery is no longer seen as **(e)** .... the top international chefs are actually men. It is a highly competitive industry and one with vast opportunities. Recent media coverage has had a large impact on this, where 'cooking' is no longer associated with gender and just the home. Programmes covering all aspects of food hygiene, the catering industry and competitions **(f)** .... are shown every day on the television. So why not make our home economics class compulsory?

Adapted from*: *www.scmp.com

D Writing

1 Students at your school have been informed that they might be starting cookery classes.

Write an email to your head teacher, telling them your feelings about this. Here are two comments from your friends.

'I don't think cookery is relevant in school today. Who needs to cook?'

'I'm very excited that cooking classes are going to start. We spend far too much time doing non-practical subjects.'

Write the email to your head teacher.

The comments above may give you some ideas, and you can also use some ideas of your own.

Your email should be between 150 and 200 words long. You will receive up to 8 marks for the content of your email, and up to 8 marks for the language.

....

....

....

....

....

....

....

....

....

....

....

....

Unit 19

Fashions

A Vocabulary

1 Find the word which has two meanings. Sometimes the word is two different parts of speech.

Example: A symbol in the alphabet (noun) L E T T E R. A written or typed communication (noun)

- **a** Create fabric using thread with this method (verb) _ _ _ _ _. A way to walk unhindered through many people (verb)
- **b** To cut very short (verb) _ _ _ _. A type of cultivated plant like cereals or fruit (noun)
- **c** Part of shoe that raises foot from the ground (noun) _ _ _ _ _ _ _ _. Where you wait for a train (noun)
- **d** From the beginning, without using anything that exists (noun) _ _ _ _ _ _ _. To rub your skin with your nails, often to stop it itching (verb)
- **e** A place to go away from the sun (noun) _ _ _ _ _. The lightness or darkness of a colour (noun)
- **f** The small green parts of a tree (noun) _ _ _ _ _ _. Goes away from somewhere (verb)
- **g** A type of citrus fruit (noun) _ _ _ _ _ _. A colour (noun)
- **h** An outdoor place to sell goods (noun) _ _ _ _ _ _. To advertise or promote something (verb)
- **i** Belonging to the present time (adjective) _ _ _ _ _ _ _. Flow of electricity (noun)
- **j** A sports shoe (noun) _ _ _ _ _ _ _. A person who coaches others (noun)
- **k** Colloquial word for clothing (noun) _ _ _ _. Controls the speed in a car (noun)
- **l** A domesticated animal (noun) _ _ _. To stroke or caress an animal (verb)
- **m** Everything the same (adjective)_ _ _ _ _ _ _. Clothes worn by students at school (noun)

2 Match the words and phrases to form phrases from Unit 19. Some variations are possible.

a ~~Ethnic~~	**g** An atmosphere of	**i** gear	**vii** pride
b Ethical	**h** Erase their	**ii** ridicule	**viii** engineering
c Alternative	**i** Sweeping the	**iii** fashions	**ix** nation
d Design and	**j** The latest	**iv** ~~minority groups~~	**x** individuality
e Latest	**k** Designer	**v** styles	**xi** peer-pleasing designs
f Avoid	**l** Academic	**vi** fashion	**xii** results

a *iv*	**d**	**g**	**j** ....
b	**e**	**h**	**k** ....
c	**f**	**i**	**l** ....

3 Check your answers to Exercise A2 and then use the phrases to complete these sentences.

- **a** There was .... amongst the students about how much money had been raised.
- **b** Many of the .... were given special tuition to improve their English.
- **c** If you stopped making such a fool of yourself, then maybe you would ....
- **d** The .... were not very good this year in the practical exams.
- **e** .... of music were played to represent all the different people.
- **f** Because many children are exploited in the production of clothes an awareness of .... has become 'fashionable'.
- **g** She is thinking of studying .... at university next year.
- **h** You have to buy the .... if you want to join the club.
- **i** Many people feel that school uniforms .... because everyone looks the same.
- **j** A feeling of patriotism is .... during the football competition.
- **k** .... can be very expensive because you pay for the name.
- **l** Fashion is for others, not for yourself, with the ....

4 Complete the sentences using either *global* or *world*.

- **a** There has been a .... recession since the fall in the price of oil.
- **b** Both starvation and obesity are .... issues which exist in different parts of the ....
- **c** The .... has become a much smaller place with the popularity of budget airlines.
- **d** Do you believe in life on another planet or a .... similar to ours?
- **e** There are many .... problems that we need to solve together.
- **f** Over 2000 years ago people used to believe that the .... was flat.

B Language focus: position of adjectives

1 Use the following adjectives to complete each sentence.

hand-spun	fermented	contemporary	traditional	complex	alternative
businesslike	mandatory	global	fashionable	domesticated	personal

- **a** A cat that enjoys living in a home and knows how to behave is ....
- **b** If it's a decision that you have no choice in, then it's ....
- **c** If you have a choice, then it offers you an ....

d If your clothes are up to date, then you are ....

e If a textile goes through the process of being made by hand, then it is ....

f If a crossword is difficult or not simple to do, then it is ....

g If a problem, like pollution, relates to the whole world, then it is ....

h When the juice of a plant, fruit or vegetable goes through a chemical process, then this means it is ....

i If an issue concerns only you and is not public, then it's ....

j If you have a practical and professional approach to your work, then you are ....

k If you are conventional and use long-established practices, then you are ....

l Modern art and fashion are also known as ....

2 Above were examples of verb + adjective. Now write the phrases as adjective + noun.

Example: a domesticated cat

b ....

c ....

d ....

e ....

f ....

g ....

h ....

i ....

j ....

k ....

l ....

3 Find three more examples of adjective + noun and verb + adjective in Unit 19 of your Coursebook.

a .... **d** ....

b .... **e** ....

c .... **f** ....

4 Use your examples in Exercise B3 to write complete sentences.

a ....

b ....

c ....

d ....

e ....

C Skills

Listening

1 You are going to listen to an interview from the fashion industry and will hear the following words. What do they mean? Use paper or digital reference sources to help you and write the definition for each one.

a fibre ....

b spin ....

c thread ....

d weave ....

e cloth ....

2 Look at the image of the jacket. Where are the hood, collar and pocket flap?

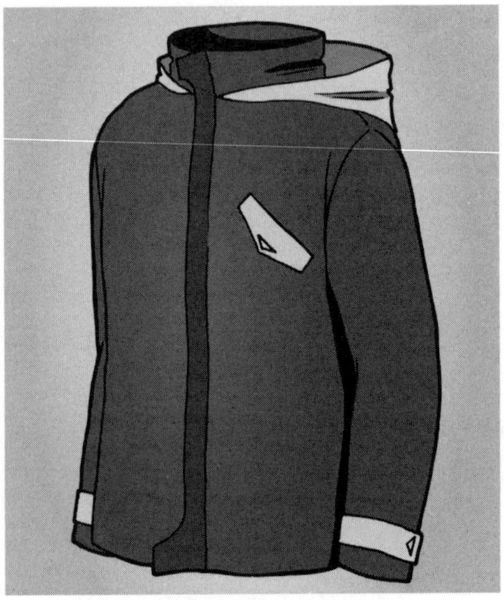

3 You are going to listen to an interview with a designer who is working with two companies to manufacture a range of jackets with mobile phone and MP3 technology. First read the questions below and identify the key word/s in each one. Decide exactly what information is being asked for. Now, predict an answer for each question. Write your predicted answer.

a What has changed about clothing over the years?

....

....

....

b How many basic stages are there in the clothes-making process?

....

c What roles do the three partners have?

....

d Where in the new jackets will the earphones be?

....

e What will happen when the phone rings?

....

f How are the phone and the MP3 player controlled?

....

g Where does Conte get the ideas for his clothes from?

....

h What type of garments form the majority of Conte's collection?

....

i What does Conte hope to include in his future designs?

....

j What would be the **two** benefits of face-recognition cameras?

....

k Why do you think the interviewer asks if Conte's designs will look fashionable?

....

4 **CD2, Track 24** Now listen to the interview and write your answers. Check your predictions in Exercise C3 and make any necessary changes.

5 Complete the notes below by writing one or two words only in each gap.

Technology tomorrow – the clothes industry

a Clothes fibres have changed, but clothes-making process is same: spinning, weaving, ... and ....

b Technical clothing to be produced by GHK Electrics and the Jeane Company, range of ...., designed by Giovanni Conte, and soon available in shops.

c Jackets will have phones with .... technology, microphone and earphones in hood or ....

d .... controls everything, hidden under pocket flap.

e If dirty, jacket can be washed in ....

f Conte gets ideas from all over the world, has in excess of .... items in his Bologna studio, which inspire his designs.

g Future designs could include .... for face-recognition with technology .... in the fabric, and therefore ....

h Clothes will still be .... and will not look like clothes from ....

6 **CD2, Track 24** You can now listen again to check your answers.

Unit 20
Technology

A Vocabulary

1 What is the missing word in each of the following ten great technological inventions?

a a mobile ....

b .... connectivity

c global positioning ....

d personal ....

e computer ....

f .... camera

g remote ....

h .... oven

i digital ....

j video ....

2 Which invention from Exercise A1 does each piece of information below refer to?

a a 30-ton monster ....

b information dissemination and communication ....

c instantaneous and untethered communication ....

d modernised the way we eat ....

e news dissemination and recording history ....

f sound quality and sharing ability ....

g tail-like cord and round body ....

h talking face to face ....

i wirelessly change the TV channel ....

j you will never get lost again ....

3 In Unit 20 you read about (i) self-lacing trainers, (ii) aerial wind turbines, (iii) smart fridges, (iv) an airport control centre. For each of these four topics, think of **three** connected words or phrases.

(i) self-lacing trainers	(ii) aerial wind turbines	(iii) smart fridges	(iv) airport control centres
tightens the shoe	*electricity*		

4 In which of the same four texts did you read the following phrases? There are **three** phrases for each text.

Example: 200 000 passengers (iv) airport control centres

- **a** a team of engineers ....
- **b** above the clouds ....
- **c** battery that lasts for about two weeks ....
- **d** biometric data ....
- **e** correct cooking time ....
- **f** embedded wifi ....
- **g** floor-to-ceiling radar screen ....
- **h** plus and minus buttons on the side ....
- **i** six megawatts ....
- **j** the supermarket aisle ....
- **k** underwater noise ....

5 Choose **two** of the four topics. Using the words and phrases from Exercises A1 and A2, write a short paragraph of about 50 words for each topic.

....

....

....

....

....

....

....

6 Use the correct form of either *internal* or *inside* to complete the following sentences.

- **a** He had injuries to his arms and legs as well as some .... parts of his body.
- **b** 'Is Jan in the garden?' 'No, he's ....'
- **c** Who knows what goes on .... his head?
- **d** The bank decided to have an .... investigation into the robbery.
- **e** This medicinal cream should not be taken ....
- **f** It's safer to keep your wallet in the .... pocket of your jacket.
- **g** Maria, you've got your T-shirt on .... out.
- **h** Because it is such a large country, there are many .... flights in Saudi Arabia.

B Language focus: compound subjects, introductory phrases

1 Look at these sentences from the texts you have read in Unit 20 of your Coursebook. Each one contains a compound subject. Choose a suitable verb from the box to complete the gap after each subject.

are	is	is building	loosens	monitors	tend	tightens	will tell

- **a** An adaptive lacing system that automatically .... the shoe.
- **b** Holding down the minus button for more than two seconds fully .... the shoe so that it can be removed.
- **c** The clean energy company Deepwater Wind .... a wind farm of fifteen mega turbines.
- **d** Studies show that migratory birds .... to fly near the coast.
- **e** The new, brightly coloured, hands-on appliances with embedded wifi .... too amazing to resist.
- **f** Apart from showing what is already there, the technology .... you what you can make.
- **g** Keeping the network running .... not an easy task.
- **h** In much the same way as NASA's Mission Control .... all aspects of its space exploration, the NCC manages every flight.

2 Use your own words to make complete sentences after the following compound subjects.

- **a** Even the most advanced technology in the world ....
- **b** Several hundred years in the distant past ....
- **c** Once you and your family members ....
- **d** In many different ways our lifestyles ....
- **e** Thanks to the great inventors of the past and present, ...
- **f** The whole concept of life on other planets ....

3 Use your own words to complete the following phrases.

- **a** Both Chas and Audrey ....
- **b** Honey as well as ginger ....
- **c** Neither mobile phones nor digital cameras ....
- **d** Either the manager or the team leader ....
- **e** Neither video conferencing nor internet connectivity ....
- **f** Either mobile phones or tablets ....

4 Unjumble the words to make seven key introductory phrases.

- **a** a if I have problem don't ....
- **b** even I that think don't ....
- **c** I but that believe ....

d is and the thing great ....

e not what's about like to ....

f nowadays is the that point ....

g of think can't I ....

C Skills

Reading

1 You are going to read a magazine article about useful apps for visitors in Istanbul, Turkey. Match the usage of the ten apps with the short descriptions below.

a suggests local shopping ....

b suggests best routes using public transport ....

c requests a taxi ....

d offline map ....

e a global positioning system ....

f helps find accommodation ....

g food deliveries ....

h suggests walking adventures ....

i finding out about the city ....

j finding street art ....

2 In which of the ten apps do you think you will find the following pieces of information?

a Another useful feature is a fare calculator ....

b At first glance Istanbul may not seem to offer much to hikers ....

c Filter your way through to find the kind of shop you're looking for ....

d The app has identified and listed locations in the city where you can spot the best graffiti ....

e The best thing about the app is that, unlike most other apps, your phone doesn't need to be connected to the internet to use it ....

f There are hundreds if not thousands of apps to find hotels ....

g This is a great app for those who like discovering the city in a spontaneous way ....

h Tracking buses, trams, ferries and metro in real time and detecting traffic jams ....

i Traffic is probably the main cause of nervous breakdowns in the city ....

j Whether you're craving durum, pizzas, lahmacun, burgers, tantuni, meze or sushi ....

3 Quickly read the text and check your answers to Exercises C1 and C2.

10 life-saving apps when living in Istanbul

App 1: The must-have app for getting your favourite food delivered to your door. Whether you're craving durum, pizzas, lahmacun, burgers, tantuni, meze or sushi, a delivery person will jump on their scooter and slalom around the city's traffic to get your meal to you in 30 minutes or so. It has proven so popular that locals and expats would be panicking without it.

App 2: Traffic is probably the main cause of nervous breakdowns in the city and the reason why we shouldn't blame cabdrivers for not always obeying the non-smoking rule. Like a smart GPS helping you find the best routes through traffic, this app might be your best solution to remain psychologically sane while driving your way through the crazy traffic.

App 3: This app uses your exact location to find the closest taxi and calls the driver with a single touch. It's practical, simple and offers payment choices such as cash or other credit sources. Another useful feature is a fare calculator, which can help ensure that the driver doesn't take you (and your wallet) for a spin.

App 4: This is a great app for those who like discovering the city in a spontaneous way without having to spend the whole stay with their nose stuck in a guidebook. All you need to do is to put on your headphones and enjoy the fascinating stories of lesser-known buildings of Istanbul. There's even an offline feature that allows you to use the app without an internet connection.

App 5: At first glance Istanbul might not seem to offer much to hikers, but the city is full of gems best seen on foot. This app includes a number of routes categorised thematically, so you can visit all the city's main attractions without having to hop on a tour bus. If you are feeling extra-adventurous, you can even create an original path and upload it for others to visit.

App 6: Trafi is a super-accurate app to find your way around the city with public transport. Tracking buses, trams, ferries and metro in real time and detecting traffic jams, it helps you to make the best choices when it comes to choosing a route and a mode of transport to go from A to B.

App 7: Street art has become part of the city's visual landscape with stunning murals on both sides of the Bosphorus, though these artworks are not always easy to find. The app has identified and listed locations in the city where you can spot the best graffiti with info on the local and sometimes international street artists behind them.

App 8: It's almost mission impossible to find your way in the impressive maze that is the Grand Bazaar and its shops. Worry no more. Filter your way through to find the kind of shop you're looking for, get info on the nearest ATMs and exchange office, save your favourite places to make your shopping experience at the Grand Bazaar much less overwhelming.

App 9: There are hundreds if not thousands of apps to find hotels, but this one is particularly effective because it is based in Turkey and is designed to find rooms at the last minute. So, if you urgently need a place to stay, this app could be just what you need.

App 10: While not exactly mind-blowing, this app could prove very handy when out and about in the city. It has the usual info about the city's famous landmarks, the nearest shops, restaurants and hotels, and provides useful insider tips. The best thing about the app is that, unlike most other apps, your phone doesn't need to be connected to the internet to use it.

Adapted from*: *www.timeoutistanbul.com

D Listening

1 **CD2, Track 25** You are going to listen to Hakan and Gamze, two Turkish teenagers who live in Istanbul, talking about apps. As you listen, decide which of the apps you have read about would be most suitable for them. There are two apps for each speaker.

Hakan .... and ....

Gamze .... and ....

E Writing

1 Think of an app that you would like to have on a phone or tablet. Give the app a name, and then write a short description of its features. Write 60–70 words.

....

....

....

....

2 You were recently on a school trip to a major city where you and your classmates had to use an app.

Write an email to a family member about what happened.

In your email you should:

- explain where you were and what you were doing
- say which app you had to use and why
- describe how the app helped you.

The pictures may give you some ideas, and you should try to use some ideas of your own.

Your email should be between 100–150 words (Core) or 150–200 words (Extended) long.

You will receive up to 6 (Core) / 8 (Extended) marks for the content of your email, and up to 6 (Core) / 8 (Extended) marks for the style and accuracy of your language.

....

....

....

....

....

....

....

....

....

Unit 4: C Skills: Listening [CD2, Track 18]

Narrator 1: Well I've been driving my boda boda for 15 years now and it has provided me and my family with a comfortable living. I'm a properly licensed driver and we get a lot of benefits. But in my town, Kampala, there are so many drivers who are not licensed and they are a real danger both to themselves and everyone else. So many foreigners have accidents here as they think it's great fun to rush around on a boda boda, and I just can't believe they go for any driver, often unfortunately with unexpected consequences. It's just not worth it – pay a shilling or more extra and get a trained driver, and wear a helmet which fits properly. But I love my life as a boda boda driver as it's so free and I've got to know my city so well: the smells, the type of people in each area, the best roads; all in a day's work.

Narrator 2: I came to Uganda for work and had my first boda boda experience from the airport where I was taken to my hotel along with my 25 kilo suitcase on the back of my friend's boda boda. Well, he became my friend after that nail-biting experience, as I kept throwing my arms around him because I was so frightened. We wove in and out of traffic, people, animals, other boda bodas. On my bike, one passenger and a suitcase; on other bikes four passengers! Huge bales of hay! One man sitting with a goat across his knee! Another, with a woman balancing two young children and a pair of chickens! Once I even saw a tiny new-born baby and its mother being taken from the hospital to their home – can you imagine what could have happened? I dread to think about it.

Narrator 3: I had a couple of days in Kampala and the hotel recommended that I should ride with Dennis because he was the best person to help me get to know the city. He was brilliant and I had no idea that Kampala was such an interesting and vast place. Dennis took me to all the best parts and told me so much about the history and the people who live in Kampala; I couldn't have learnt more in a better way than I did in those three days. There were six of us in total travelling together, and we just let Dennis and his five colleagues decide on our agenda and what and where we would go each day. On day one we covered some of the main sights, including the Uganda Museum which told us all about the country's history from the Stone Age until today. We went to the Lubiri Palace on day two, an amazing place with plenty of history. On the third day we left the city to see the countryside, which was truly beautiful – thank you, Dennis, you gave us a great time.

Narrator 4: I live and work in rural Uganda as a nurse and I'm like an ambulance on two wheels. We take people, especially pregnant mothers, from their homes to the local hospital. When I first started my job, what surprised me more than anything was how much trust people put in you – the patient and their families depend totally on you to get the sick person to the hospital on time. The pressure is constantly nagging me as I'm driving quickly, but not too quickly, avoiding all the potholes in the roads, the animals and children that keep running across your path, the deep puddles from the night's rainfall and so many other obstacles that can make the journey both for myself and for my passenger an extremely stressful one. But the feeling of elation when we arrive safely and I've delivered the patient to the doctors and nurses is amazing. I know that I've just done a good job.

Unit 5: C Skills: Speaking [CD2, Track 19]

Aphrodite: I've got my speaking exam next week and I'm worried about the first part. I don't feel that I can prepare properly for it. What can I do?

Teacher: Let me think ... Of course, worrying won't help! In fact, you **can** prepare because the questions you'll be asked are personal ones and are not there to challenge you.

A: To be honest, I can't feel comfortable when I'm being assessed!

T: Well, the first part of the speaking is **not** assessed, so you can relax!

A: But what if I'm asked something and I don't know how to reply in English? Can I say it in my own language?

T: No, of course not! If you don't understand something, the best thing to do is to say so. Now, what exactly would you say if you don't understand?

A: Hmmmm ... 'I'm sorry but I don't understand what you mean.'

T: Excellent! Anything else?

A: Let me think. What about 'Could you repeat that please?' or 'Could you say that more slowly please?'

T: Fantastic! Much better to let the other person know you are having difficulties by using a correct English phrase than saying nothing at all.

A: Thanks, that's good advice. But you know, I'm really worried that I'm going to be so nervous and just dry up, and not have enough to say.

T: To be honest, it is very important to keep speaking but the other person will be aware that students get nervous and of course they will help you out.

A: How?

T: Well, the other person will have some questions ready to help you.

A: What if I don't know anything about the topic?

T: Actually, you're not being tested on your knowledge of the world but on your ability to communicate in English. So, if you are asked about a topic you feel uncomfortable with, for example about global warming, then you could say 'Actually, I don't feel I know very much about global warming but one thing I am aware of, which is connected, is the water problem in my country ….'

A: Hmmm, that's great, thank you. What about my pronunciation and my accent? I sound horrible! I feel I speak so differently to the people I hear on the news and on television.

T: To be honest, nobody is asking you to have the perfect accent of a native speaker. The important thing is to speak clearly so that another person can understand you. I have no problem understanding you, so no need to worry!

A: Will I get a lower mark if I keep making mistakes?

T: Well, you will be penalised if you make too many mistakes, particularly if the mistakes make it difficult for you to be understood.

A: And what about my vocabulary? Do I know enough words?

T: Actually, with both pronunciation and vocabulary you need to speak and read as much as you can, both inside and outside the classroom.

A: Thanks for all the advice.

Unit 9: **C** Skills: Listening [CD2, Track 20]

Speaker 1: I was living in France at the time because my parents and my two older sisters were working there, and so my interview for a place at a UK university had to be done online. I was absolutely petrified about the interviewers seeing me online, because I hate being photographed. I wonder how nervous I would've been if I'd been sitting in the same room as them! But I must've looked pretty much OK because they offered me a place and I spent three very happy years studying there.

Speaker 2: I went for several university interviews and for most I was incredibly nervous. Five unsmiling faces waiting to interview me didn't help. For one interview, I had a pen in my hand which I kept rolling over my face because of my nerves. Without realising it, I had been drawing on my face, and I didn't realise until afterwards when I saw my face in the mirror! I wish now that I'd taken a photograph! Not one of the interviewers said a word!

Speaker 3: My worst experience for a university interview was the wrong place, wrong date, wrong time. Unbelievable! To this day I still don't know how I managed to get everything so terribly wrong, even though I keep going over everything in my head again and again and again. I guess perhaps I just had so much on my mind at the time that I got things mixed up. But I learnt a good lesson – never set off for an interview without checking and re-checking all the details!

Speaker 4: While I was having my university interview, one of the interviewers had a sneezing attack. At first, I managed to ignore it, but then I started to laugh and I didn't know what to do to stop myself. The situation only got worse as she continued sneezing every minute or so, and I felt incredibly rude for behaving like that. The other interviewer just continued the interview, ignoring his colleague as if these sneezing fits were a common occurrence. He dealt with it far better than I had done.

Speaker 5: My first interview for a university place is next week. I'm 100% prepared, and I've been online to check what I should and shouldn't do and say. I've also spoken to some of my teachers about how to approach the interview, and both my older sister and brother have already been through the same experience, so they also helped me get ready. I'm not sure what else I can do now, other than to be myself and try not to get too nervous, despite all my preparations.

Speaker 6: My worst university interview experience was one in which I was interviewed and filmed with seven others. We had to complete several tasks together. The idea, so they said, was to judge how we work with other people, but I felt it was very unfair. I'm not an outgoing person so I hardly said anything, while the dominant characters just kept talking non-stop. The interviewers just let us get on with it for about 20 minutes. To my great surprise, they offered me a place!

Unit 14: **D** Listening [CD2, Track 21]

A modern matron: My cousin's enthusiasm for nursing convinced me to leave banking and start a nursing diploma. My first placement in elderly care was fascinating: the patients were as interested in me as I was in them. Midwifery was exciting, as I knew nothing about childbirth. Before I finished my diploma I was already planning my career.

I wanted a challenging speciality where I'd really get to know my patients. Mental health seemed perfect: the patients love to talk, and the nurses don't wear uniforms. I like people knowing who I am purely by the way I handle myself.

To gain the right skills, I studied part time for my nursing degree and then took a Master's in Transcultural Psychiatry, which gave me an insight into how mental disorders and their treatment can be influenced by cultural and ethnic factors. I also spent a year as a unit manager in a private hospital, which really opened my eyes to financial management.

Two years later, these skills helped bring me to my current position as modern matron for a mental health unit. People lose so much when they suffer from mental illness: jobs, relationships, physical health, even the ability to look after themselves. It's incredibly satisfying to help someone get their life back, watch them regain their skills and give them hope and aspirations.

Friends of mine in accounting and banking say they've never changed someone's life for the better. I have. On Sundays, they dread going to work the next day. I can't wait.

A relief community nurse: My second child had just been born when I discovered a nursing course was starting nearby. Having worked in nursing homes and been frustrated by the limited level of care I could give, this seemed too good to pass up.

I began the course shortly after my baby was born and then took the chance to gain a lifelong career.

My first year as a qualified nurse was on a busy cancer ward, caring for acutely ill patients. I quickly learnt to manage my workload to stay focused on patient care, and to think on my feet. It was very challenging meeting new patients, managing chemotherapy and handling all the physical, social and emotional issues that accompany it. Incredibly rewarding too, but you have to be extremely organised to coordinate the high volume of testing, monitoring and treatment cancer patients need.

After such an intense environment, I spent the next year in orthopaedic outpatients with high numbers of less acute patients. It was a good chance to experience a very different style of nursing in a different setting.

Now I'm doing something completely different again, as a relief community nurse. Each morning I go to an assigned location anywhere in my area and pick up my caseload. In a typical morning I'll visit up to eight patients in their own home, a clinic or a nursing home. No two days are alike.

Community nursing is a world away from hospital nursing. Observing and listening to patients in their own environment can help you pick up on other relevant issues. Every day, your knowledge, teaching and influencing skills are tested as you educate patients about the consequences of their choices. To anyone considering nursing as a career, I'd say try it: get some experience so you are realistic about what to expect.

Adapted from: nursing.nhscareers.nhs.uk

Unit 15: B Language focus: quantifiers, fillers – Exercise 3 [CD2, Track 22]

Layla: To be honest, I don't think I have a particularly healthy lifestyle nowadays. I guess that I'm too busy at school, doing homework, and helping out at home. But I know that I should do more. The longer you wait, the more difficult it gets to change. In addition, and having said that, I think my diet is pretty healthy, and I play sports at school and walk everywhere. It could be worse!

Sara: Some of my school friends have a healthy lifestyle. They are very keen on sports and play in different school teams. They all say how much they enjoy it, and they never seem to be bored with nothing to do. Furthermore, they quite often ask me to join in, but I fear I won't be as good as them and make a fool of myself.

Hana: Obviously a healthy lifestyle makes you feel better. But in my opinion a healthy lifestyle can also be expensive. I think the key is moderation. If you do the right amount, it is obviously very beneficial, but too much could cause an injury. So it's probably not a bad idea to programme your healthy lifestyle, by firstly including both physical and mental activity, and secondly introducing a balanced diet.

Miska: It seems to me that if you are really interested and involved in something I think it can become stressful and dangerous. This type of lifestyle can take over everything you do, and I think that can be risky and cause you to worry. Is it worth it? I don't think so. There's no need to be extreme about living in a healthy way. I'm young and I want to enjoy my life!

Adam: I believe that health and fitness is a business like any other, and people have to profit from it. I think that when you pay for something, it's up to you to make sure you are getting good value for money. There are cheats and people who want to make more and more everywhere, and the health and fitness scene is no different. I'm afraid there's nothing you can do about it.

Unit 15: D Listening [CD2, Track 23]

George: So, this topic is about lifestyle changes. What do you think, Caroline? Any ideas?

Caroline: Well, it's a good topic for me. I believe it's important to have a healthy lifestyle, and I can think of quite a lot to say.

G: For example? What about the first prompt: *things that you have today that people one hundred years ago had no idea about.* What are your thoughts on that?

C: Well, I guess the internet has given us far more information than we used to have, so it's easy to find out about our ancestors and what they had. Of course, technology has changed our lives dramatically in a very short time, but my great-grandparents use social media all the time, and are very confident about it.

G: Same here. Even though my great-grandma is nearly 90, she sends me a message every so often, and I know that every weekend she chats online to her family in New Zealand. Really incredible, isn't it?!

C: What do you think about the second prompt: *your idea of a healthy lifestyle compared to your grandparents' lifestyles?* I think our great-grandparents are examples of people who have had a healthy lifestyle.

G: I agree. If they had had an unhealthy lifestyle, they wouldn't be as active as they currently are. Amazing, really. The third prompt is: *standards of living and differences in income and* *possessions*. How do you think those have changed in the past one hundred years, Caroline?

C: I think today we have too many possessions. Our homes are full of things that we don't need and definitely don't use. We're constantly buying things just because we can, not because we really need them. It's difficult to comprehend.

G: I don't think that having lots of possessions improves our standard of living. For many people it's just about showing off.

C: You're right. What do you think about number four: *opportunities to know more about healthy living and different lifestyles?* Like I said before, you just need to search online and there's so much information. Too much probably.

G: Yes, but also at school nowadays we have far more opportunities to learn about healthy living and different lifestyles. I think those lessons are really interesting and very important for young people today.

C: OK. For the last prompt: *the idea that people in the past had a much better understanding of a healthy lifestyle than we do today,* I'm not sure that I agree at all.

G: Me too. I think we are just as aware today, perhaps even more so.

C: Yes, but the difference is that today many people choose to ignore what they know is the right thing to do, they ignore the information.

G: OK, we're done!

Unit 19: C Skills: Listening [CD2, Track 24]

Clothing Technology

Last week, our fashion and style reporter, Tammy Smith, spent some time with Giovanni Conte, who was last year voted the most influential designer of the millennium (so far ...!). Here's what happened when they met up in the Royal Hotel ...

Tammy Smith: Giovanni, is it true that the clothes industry is technically backward?

Giovanni Conte: Most definitely! For example, although the actual fibres we use in producing materials have changed considerably over the centuries, the clothes-making process itself is basically the same: spin the fibre into thread, weave the thread into cloth, cut it into pieces and then sew it back together again to make an item of clothing. Very simple, really.

TS: But I understand all this is about to change, isn't it?

GC: That's my plan, yes, and it's incredibly exciting. I've got together with GHK Electrics and the Jeane Company to produce a range of technical clothing. We have incorporated GHK mobile-phone and MP3 technology into a range of jackets designed by me and made by the Jeane Company.

TS: But mobile-phone and MP3 technology incorporated into clothes? How does that work?

GC: Well, the jackets, which will soon be available in shops all over the world, will feature phones which can be dialled using voice-recognition technology, and a microphone and earphones built into the hood or collar.

The MP3 player automatically cuts out when the phone rings, like on an aircraft when an announcement is made. Everything is controlled via a keypad hidden beneath a pocket flap.

TS: But what happens when the jacket gets dirty?

GC: The whole range is totally machine-washable and very fast-drying.

TS: Where do you get your design ideas from?

GC: Over the years, I've collected clothes from all over the world and, in my studio in Bologna, I have built up a wardrobe of more than 50 000 garments, mostly military uniforms, which provide me with inspiration for my designs.

TS: Apart from the phone and MP3 player, what else could be incorporated into your designs?

GC: Currently, I am looking into the possibility of building in a face-recognition camera, which would provide you with information about a person when you meet them again. Parents could keep an eye on their children through miniature cameras. And all this technology would be invisible, submerged in the fabric. It won't be long before all clothes contain some sort of micro-computer.

TS: But with all this in-built technology, will clothes still look fashionable?

GC: But of course! It's very important that clothes look beautiful, so I have tried to achieve the right balance between fashion and usefulness, just as the Jeane Company first did in 1874. My designs do not look like clothes from space!

Unit 20: D Listening [CD2, Track 25]

Gamze: I need something to help me get around town quickly and without having to wait too long for transport, and I want to be able to pay in cash or online if I've run out of money. Also, I want to know in advance how much I'm going to have to pay, if possible. Do you think there's an app to do that for me?

Hakan: I'm sure there are some to choose from. Me, I'm more interested in sightseeing. Even though I live in Istanbul, I really don't think I know enough about its history, so I want an app that will show me all those hidden places. I don't want to have to be connected to the internet all the time, and if I can avoid having to stare at my phone screen, that would be great.

G: What else? I'd like an app for shopping, something that will guide me through the biggest market in Istanbul. Even though I live here in this city, I always get lost inside the market.

H: Me too! It's impossible! My other must-have app is for finding my way around the city itself. Like you, I was born and grew up here, but the city is changing so rapidly that sometimes I don't recognise places. Obviously I don't drive yet but I love walking, so an app that shows me all the best places, and without having to be online would be great.

Acknowledgements

The authors and publishers acknowledge the following sources of copyright material and are grateful for the permissions granted. While every effort has been made, it has not always been possible to identify the sources of all the material used, or to trace all copyright holders. If any omissions are brought to our notice, we will be happy to include the appropriate acknowledgements on reprinting.

Text

Unit 1 adapted from article '7 Ways Successful People Spend Their Free Time' by Jayson DeMers, reproduced by permission; Unit 2 adapted from article 'The State of Television, Worldwide' by Tom Butts, 6 December 2013, Copyrighted 2016, TV Technology, (125338:1016RR), reproduced by permission; Unit 4 excerpts from '10 Unusual Types of Transport' by Holly Dudley (https://www.roughguides.com/article/10-unusual-types-of-transport/#ixzz464YHhB6I), Copyright © Rough Guides, 2012, reproduced by permission of Penguin Books Ltd.; Unit 6 'What's the danger for video-game players?' adapted from Video Game Addiction: Physical Consequences of Gaming Addiction from www.video-game-addiction.org, reprinted by permission of CRC Health; Unit 8 adapted from article 'We have abandoned our children to the Internet' by Beeban Kidron, 13 September 2013, Copyright Guardian News & Media Ltd. 2013, reproduced by permission; Unit 11 'Which person…?' adapted from article 'Great Achievements by Teenagers' from www.conservapedia.com; Unit 12 text from the website of the Black Jaguar White Tiger Foundation blackjaguarwhitetiger.org/about-us; Unit 13 'Felix Baumgartner: watch the jump', October 2012, © Telegraph Media Group Limited 2012; Unit 14 NHS Careers, real life stories are from www.healthcareers.nhs.uk used under the Open Government Licence; Unit 15 'Dealing with asthma triggers' adapted from KidsHealth.org © The Nemours Foundation/KidsHealth, reprinted with permission; Unit 16 adapted from article 'Twitter overtakes Facebook as the most popular social network for teens, according to study' by Alex Greig, 24 October 2013, Daily Mail, reproduced by permission of Solo Syndication; Unit 17 adapted from 'What does climate change mean to young people?' October 2013, reprinted by permission of RTCC (Responding to Climate Change); Unit 18 'Should cooking be taught at school?' adapted from article by Chan Chi Man, Cathy, in The South China Morning Post; Unit 20 '10 life-saving apps when living in Istanbul' adapted from p. 48 of Time Out Istanbul, May 2015, reprinted by permission of Time Out England Limited.

Images

Cover image Mark Wragg/Getty Images; U4D(1) Sergiy Kuzmin/Shutterstock U12C(1a) Kevin Schafer/Minden Pictures/Getty Images; U12C(1b) Barry Bland/Barcroft Media/Getty Images; U12C(1c) Joel Sartore/Getty Images; U12C(1d) Dave King/Getty Images; U13C(1a) Frazer Harrison/Getty Images; U13C(1b) ALEXANDER KLEIN/AFP/Getty Images; U15C White Packert/Getty Images.